WILD MOUTH

WILD
MOUTH

For Sue —
Thank you for your
valued friendship —
Much love,
Maureen
'08

MAUREEN HUNTER

Wild Mouth
first published 2008 by
Scirocco Drama
An imprint of J. Gordon Shillingford Publishing Inc.
© 2008 Maureen Hunter

Scirocco Drama Editor: Glenda MacFarlane
Cover design by Terry Gallagher/Doowah Design Inc.
Author photo by Earl Kennedy
Printed and bound in Canada on 100% post-consumer recycled paper.

We acknowledge the financial support of the Manitoba Arts Council, The Canada
Council for the Arts and the Government of Canada through the Book Publishing
Industry Development Program (BPIDP) for our publishing program.

Production inquiries should be addressed to:
Charles W. Northcote
Core Literary Inc.
140 Wolfrey Avenue
Toronto, ON M4K 1L3
charlesnorthcote@rogers.com
Ph 416-466-4929

Library and Archives Canada Cataloguing in Publication

Hunter, Maureen, 1947-
    Wild mouth / Maureen Hunter.

A play.
ISBN 978-1-897289-27-3

    I. Title.

PS8565.U5814W54 2008   C812'.54   C2008-903879-7

J. Gordon Shillingford Publishing
P.O. Box 86, RPO Corydon Avenue, Winnipeg, MB Canada R3M 3S3

For Stephen McDermott Fowles
a soldier of the Great War
whose spirit called out to me

and for
Doug Evans and R.H. Thomson
with gratitude

Maureen Hunter

Saskatchewan-born, Winnipeg-based Maureen Hunter is one of Canada's most accomplished playwrights. Her work has been produced extensively on Canada's major stages, as well as in Britain and the U.S., and by CBC and BBC Radio. It has been nominated for two Governor General's Awards, two Dora Mavor Moore Awards (Outstanding New Play) and the Lou Siminovitch Prize in Theatre.

Wild Mouth, Hunter's latest play, premiered at Tarragon Theatre, Toronto, in January 2008. Other plays include *Vinci*, premiered by the National Arts Centre, Ottawa, in co-production with Manitoba Theatre Centre in 2002; *Atlantis*, premiered in English by MTC/Theatre Calgary in 1996 and in French by Théâtre de la Manufacture, Montreal, in 1999; and *Transit of Venus*, which received its Canadian premiere at MTC in 1992 and a year later became the first Canadian play ever staged by the Royal Shakespeare company of Britain. It received its U.S. premiere in 1998 at the Berkshire Theatre in Stockbridge, Mass. In November 2007, Manitoba Opera premiered *Transit of Venus* as a full-length opera, composed by Victor Davies with a libretto by Maureen.

Other plays include *Footprints on the Moon*, *Beautiful Lake Winnipeg* and *I Met a Bully on the Hill* (co-written with Martha Brooks). Maureen's plays have been published individually and in a number of anthologies.

Characters

Anna, 45
Logan, 60, her brother
Roberta, 55, her sister-in-law
Claire, 19, her niece
Jamie, 15, her nephew
Aloysius, 70, Logan's hired man
Bohdan, 35, a soldier returned from the war

Setting

A farm and a coulee some distance from the fictional town of Standfast, Saskatchewan. Harvest, 1917.

Production Credits

Wild Mouth premiered at Tarragon Theatre, Toronto, on January 9, 2008 with the following cast:

ANNA..Sarah Orenstein
LOGAN..Ian D. Clark
ROBERTA .... Brenda Robins
CLAIRE...Sarah Allen
JAMIE.. Simon Rainville
ALOYSIUS..David Fox
BOHDAN .... Oliver Becker

Directed by R.H. Thomson
Set and Costume Design by Yannik Larivée
Lighting Design by Michelle Ramsay
Sound Design by Todd Charlton
Stage Manager: Alison Peddie
Assistant Director: Kate Cayley
Fight Directors: John Stead and James Binkley
Apprentice Stage Manager: Lindsay Marriner
Script Coordinator: Mary Fraser

Playwright's Notes and Acknowledgements

As someone raised in rural Saskatchewan, the grandchild of pioneer immigrants, I thought I'd absorbed the history of the settling of the prairies with my morning porridge. I discovered how much I had to learn when I began to research this play. I'm grateful for the fresh insights I've gained into that remarkable era. Three particularly helpful sources were *In Western Canada Before the War: Impressions of Early Twentieth Century Prairie Communities* by Elizabeth B. Mitchell; *A Flannel Shirt and Liberty: British Emigrant Gentlewomen in the Canadian West, 1880-1914*, edited by Susan Jackal; and John Herd Thompson's *The Harvests of War: The Prairie West, 1914-1918*.

Anyone who has delved into the history of the Great War is familiar with the wealth of material available on the subject. Of the many books I read, the ones that touched me most deeply were the personal accounts, particularly the collections of soldiers' letters. In *Letters from the Front: 1914-1918*, edited by John Laffin, two particular soldiers, whose names are unknown, made a great impression. One was a British artillery officer. In an unmailed letter to the girl he loved, he wrote about the soldiers' need for "women who are shameless in their pity." The other was a young French officer whose evocative letters to his mother are reflected in Alexander's letters, which Anna quotes in the play. This young man, who died in April 1915, looked at the world through an artist's eyes and dreamed of becoming one. '"It is the duty of the artist," he wrote, "to open his flowers without dread of frost." We'll never know what he might have painted, but his words are carved on my heart.

The impetus for this play I owe to a young Manitoba soldier named Stephen McDermott Fowles. It was his face in a newspaper photograph, the account of his execution in France in June 1918, and his sister's recollection of the effect of that execution on her family that propelled me into the play. Although I soon abandoned the idea of writing about an executed soldier, the notion of the impact of faraway events on a family at home caught hold.

Wild Mouth wouldn't exist in its present form without the help of two people. The first is R.H. Thomson. In addition to directing the premiere production, Robert served as dramaturg to the play from the first draft onward. His wit and wisdom, his persistence and passion for the subject, and his delightful sense of irony have shaped and enriched the work in countless ways. The other is Doug Evans, my highly unpaid research assistant. How many writers are lucky enough to have as a close personal friend a true "Renaissance man," knowledgeable on virtually every subject, with a memory like a steel trap? He has been a living resource for all my plays, helping to allay the fears and challenges of writing historical drama. I'm deeply indebted to him.

I'm grateful to Steven Schipper, Artistic Director of the Manitoba Theatre Centre, for initially commissioning *Wild Mouth* and for involving Robert as dramaturg, and to Richard Rose, Artistic Director of Tarragon Theatre, Toronto, for premiering the play and for his wisdom and guidance through the later stages of its development.

I'd like to acknowledge the assistance of the Manitoba Arts Council, Oseredok Ukrainian Cultural and Educational Centre, the actors who performed in the premiere production and those who participated in readings of the play in Winnipeg and Toronto, and the following individuals: Martha Brooks; Larry Desrochers; Leonard and Judy Harapiuk; George Kennedy; Stephanie Kostiuk; Laurie Lam; Darlene Lazenby. Thanks, as always, to Gary, my family and friends.

The lines quoted by Aloysius in Act I, Scene One are from "Resignation" by Henry Wadsworth Longfellow. The lines quoted by Roberta in Act II, Scene Two are from *A Charm* by Rudyard Kipling. The verse sung by the family at meal-times is "The Adelynrood Grace" by Elizabeth F. Lobdell, from *The Book of Common Praise*. It has been abridged. I have been unable to find the source of the grace spoken by Aloysius in Act II, Scene Seven. The concept of the seduction of violence I owe to three books in particular: Michael Herr's *Dispatches*, Anthony Lloyd's *My War Gone By, I Miss it So* and *War is a Force that Gives Us Meaning* by Chris Hedges.

Civilization is hideously fragile...
there's not much between us and the horrors underneath,
just about a coat of varnish.
— C.P. Snow

Act I

Prelude

> *Blackness. In the blackness we hear a herd of buffalo thundering across the prairie. We have only begun to understand what we're hearing when the air is filled with the sickening sounds of impact and bellows of pain as the buffalo tumble over the edge of an abyss and plunge downward to their deaths. A hawk screeches: scree! scree! scree! The sound is both human and otherworldly. The buffalo come to rest. The hawk screeches again. Then there is silence.*

Scene One

> *The kitchen of LOGAN and ROBERTA's farm home. Suppertime. LOGAN, ROBERTA, CLAIRE, JAMIE and ALOYSIUS stand at the table, singing grace. ANNA stands slightly apart.*

ALL BUT ANNA: *(Sing.)* Be present at our table, Lord. / Be everywhere adored; / Bless these thy gifts and grant that we / May with our lives thank thee.

LOGAN: For what we are about to receive, may the Lord make us truly thankful.

ROBERTA: Amen.

> *Everyone sits.*

LOGAN: What are we receiving? Roast beef!

ROBERTA: The last of it. It's chicken tomorrow, I guess.

(Passing a platter.) Anna, why don't you start?

ANNA: All right, but only for tonight. I won't be treated like
             a guest. I came to help, Roberta. I don't want an idle
             moment.

ROBERTA: You've come to the right place, then.

LOGAN: If you get fed up with the kitchen, tell you what
             we'll do. Fit you out in some overalls and put you
             to work in the barn.

JAMIE: *(Laughs.)* With a fork. You can shovel out the...

ROBERTA: Jamie.

JAMIE: Manure. I was going to say manure.

ANNA: I wouldn't mind at all. *(To JAMIE.)* I shoveled the
             stuff before you were born. Just you remember
             that.

ROBERTA: Help yourself, Aloysius.

             ALOYSIUS picks up a bowl, but offers it to ANNA.

ALOYSIUS: Mrs. McGrath.

ANNA: *(Takes the bowl.)* You haven't changed, Aloysius.

LOGAN: Talks our ears off now at mealtime.

ANNA: Aloysius?

LOGAN: The same. If you've anything to say, you'd better
             say it now. Won't get a word in later.

ROBERTA: Leave the poor man alone. It's Jamie you should be
             after. He nearly took the gatepost down, turning in
             at the lane.

LOGAN: And worked up a lather, I noticed.

JAMIE: Yeah. 'Cause the two of them seemed so
             goddamned anxious—

ROBERTA: Jamie!

JAMIE: Well, you did. *(To ANNA.)* You should have seen them before I left. The pacing, the wringing of hands! You'd think I was going to fetch the queen.

CLAIRE: She is a queen to me.

ANNA: Why, thank you, Claire. You always were my favorite niece.

JAMIE: No competition, of course.

LOGAN: *(To ANNA, indicating JAMIE.)* Keep you waiting?

ANNA: Right on time. He was tying up the horses just as the train pulled in. He's grown so tall I hardly knew him.

JAMIE: So handsome, I think you mean.

LOGAN: *(To JAMIE.)* You got the salt? And the sawdust? And picked up the papers?

JAMIE: I did. Can I read them first, for once?

LOGAN: You know the answer to that.

ROBERTA: *(To ANNA.)* I hope your room's all right. I know it isn't fancy—

ANNA: It's got a view of the coulee. What more can I ask?

ROBERTA: Claire will take up some towels for you, as soon as they're off the line.

ANNA: I've already taken a photograph. The light was exquisite just now.

LOGAN: You haven't mentioned C.L.

ANNA: C.L. who?

LOGAN: Ah.

ANNA: I hardly see him these days. And what have you been up to?

LOGAN: Oh, the usual. Lying about. Sleeping in. Admiring my stamp collection.

ANNA: The crop looks wonderful.

ROBERTA: If only we can get it off!

LOGAN: We're next in line for the threshing crew. But, I tell you! Creaky old men and spindly young boys. You'd laugh if it weren't so sad.

ANNA: You'll be glad you bought that tractor.

> *The others laugh.*

What's funny?

ROBERTA: He can't get the darn thing to run.

LOGAN: Not entirely correct.

> *JAMIE, in an undertone, makes the sound of an engine.*

In fact, I did get it running— just the other day.

JAMIE: *(In an undertone, imitating LOGAN.)* God damn bleeding—!

LOGAN: For thirty-seven seconds. That's a record, I think.

ROBERTA: They say it's the way of the future. Well, the future has not arrived!

LOGAN: It'll do the work of four horses—if I can get it off its ass.

ROBERTA: Logan.

ANNA: *(To LOGAN.)* Do you still have William's horse?

LOGAN: Trooper? Yes.

ANNA: I want to ride him. Flat out across the prairie. On a windy day!

LOGAN: Bad idea.

ANNA: Why?

JAMIE: You couldn't handle him.

ANNA: I've handled the best of them.

JAMIE: You haven't handled Trooper. Don't even try it.

ANNA: We'll see.

               Pause.

CLAIRE: You're not eating, Aunt Anna.

ANNA: I'm a little unsettled, I guess.

ROBERTA: The train will do that to you. And that old road from Standfast is as bumpy as a washboard.

ANNA: At least now it's a road. It wasn't much more than a trail, the day I first came west. *(To LOGAN.)* Remember?

LOGAN: Now why would I remember that?

ANNA: *(To CLAIRE.)* He met me at the station and tied my trunk to the buckboard and out we drove across the prairies—bouncing like peas on a shovel!—the wild wind in our faces. I clung to the seat with one hand and to my hat with the other. It was just like being at sea!

ROBERTA: *(Very dry.)* On a fairly calm day.

ANNA: I thought: so much room! Not just for the body; the soul. I felt like a prisoner, unexpectedly set free. There were hawks reeling overhead—

               JAMIE mimes drawing a bow across a fiddle. ROBERTA stops him with a look.

And herds of deer in the distance and coyotes and meadowlarks. And suddenly I knew: I'd never go back to England. The prairie had set its cap for me and by God, I was smitten!

A silence. LOGAN clears his throat.

LOGAN:　　It got Roberta just as fast.

ROBERTA:　Did it, now?

LOGAN:　　Fell for it like she fell for me.

JAMIE:　　She fell so fast for Father, he darn near had to catch her.

LOGAN:　　*(To ANNA.)* She's told you that story?

ANNA:　　What story?

LOGAN:　　She hasn't told you how we met? Well, the time has come! Go on, Roberta.

ROBERTA:　Oh! She doesn't want to hear that.

ANNA:　　Of course I do.

The telephone rings, off. It startles everyone.

LOGAN:　　*(To ROBERTA.)* Don't you get up. I'll take it.

LOGAN stands and exits. ROBERTA, CLAIRE, JAMIE and ALOYSIUS follow him with their eyes.

ROBERTA:　It's not much of a story at all. I'd gone with some friends to Blackpool. The eleventh of March, 1889.

LOGAN:　　*(Off.)* Hello?

ROBERTA:　A bitter, bone-chilling day. You had to shout to be heard over the roar of the waves.

LOGAN:　　*(Off.)* Hello?

ANNA:　　*(To ROBERTA.)* And?

ROBERTA: And... your brother was sitting there. My hat blew off. He ran and caught it.

LOGAN: *(Off.)* Who?

ROBERTA: Brought it back to me. His fingers red from the cold. He said—

LOGAN: *(Shouting, off.)* You'll have to speak up, I can't hear you!

ROBERTA: *(Distracted.)* He said...

JAMIE: *(Mimicking LOGAN.)* That's a very pretty hat. You want to hang onto that.

LOGAN: *(Off.)* Get off the line, Mrs. Scott. I know it's you, I can hear your clock chiming.

ROBERTA: He said he was from the Midlands, but he'd been eight years in Canada—

LOGAN: *(Off.)* That's better.

JAMIE: *(Again, mimicking LOGAN.)* Out in the Great Lone Land!

> *The door between LOGAN and the kitchen closes. This doesn't pass unnoticed. LOGAN is still heard intermittently, but his words are muffled.*

ANNA: He'd come back for a visit.

ROBERTA: *(With an effort.)* So he maintained. To this day he won't admit the truth. He'd come back for a wife. There were more bachelors on the prairies in those days than Beecham's got pills. No single women at all. Aloysius can vouch for that. Can't you, Aloysius?

ALOYSIUS: I can.

CLAIRE: *(To ANNA.)* They were married three weeks later in the village church. Went straight from the church to the ship!

ROBERTA: I said goodbye to my parents as though I were just
              off to Devon. No concept of the distance. No notion
              in my head of never seeing them again. *(Another
              glance at the door.)* But of course I never did.

CLAIRE: The further west they came, the emptier it got. Not
              a house for miles!

ROBERTA: But Logan was no fool. He'd planned it so we'd
              reach the homestead just as the sun went down. It
              wasn't lost on me.

CLAIRE: Then you saw your future home.

ROBERTA: Hardly more than a shack. I could feel Logan hold
              his breath. I knew whatever I said at that moment,
              it would set the tone for a lifetime. So—

              *The door to the kitchen opens and LOGAN enters.
              He shakes his head at ROBERTA.*

LOGAN: How far did you get?

ANNA: You'd just pulled up to the shack.

LOGAN: That old ramshackle thing. *(To ANNA.)* She studied
              if for the longest time. Then do you know what she
              said? Tell her, Roberta.

ROBERTA: I said—

LOGAN: *(To ANNA.)* Listen! *(To ROBERTA.)* Go on.

ROBERTA: Well! If it burns down we won't have lost much.

              LOGAN throws back his head and laughs.

LOGAN: I nearly fell off the wagon.

ROBERTA: Logan—

LOGAN: *(To ANNA.)* She told you about Blackpool, I take it?
              How I chased after her hat?

ANNA: So gallant!

LOGAN: But she didn't mention the best part, I'll wager my whiskers on that. Well? Don't anyone ask.

JAMIE: *(Picking up the cue.)* You know, Father—

LOGAN: *(To ANNA.)* I'd already picked her out. I'd seen her on the train to Blackpool. I'd followed her. I was already besotted—

ROBERTA: Listen to him!

LOGAN: —by a straw hat with a wide blue ribbon, and the girl who was wearing it. I was trying to imagine how to introduce myself, when the wind blew her straight to me.

ALOYSIUS: That was an auspicious wind.

LOGAN: *(With a smile at ROBERTA.)* It was indeed.

ROBERTA: Who was it, Logan?

LOGAN: The minister. The Laurier boy is home.

CLAIRE: Art?

ROBERTA: Just like that? No telegram?

LOGAN: *(To JAMIE.)* You didn't notice him?

JAMIE: I was busy with Aunt Anna.

LOGAN: He's gone and lost his legs.

CLAIRE: *(Softly.)* My God.

LOGAN: The minister drove him home, but he said he couldn't linger. He has a commitment this evening. *(To ROBERTA.)* He'd like us to look in on them.

ROBERTA: Tonight? But Anna's only just arrived.

ANNA: Never mind about me.

JAMIE: He took all the ribbons at sports days. Didn't he, Claire?

CLAIRE: Yes, he was quite the athlete.

JAMIE: He won't be hoofing it now.

CLAIRE: Sarah! What will she do? *(To ANNA.)* They were planning to get married as soon as he got home.

ROBERTA: Well, she can't back out of it.

CLAIRE: It's hard to imagine. She's always been so tiny and he's always been so tall!

JAMIE: A lot of fuss to go to, just to look your girl in the eye.

LOGAN: Anna.

ANNA: I hate this. I hate this!

LOGAN: Well…

ROBERTA: Fetch the cake, would you, Claire?

             CLAIRE stands and does as she's told.

             And make the tea. *(To LOGAN.)* We have time for tea?

LOGAN: If we read it now.

             ROBERTA picks up a bundle of letters. She hands one of the letters to LOGAN and sets the rest down.

ROBERTA: Look at this stack from Rosa. Why does she do this to me? I'll never have time to answer.

             CLAIRE passes plates of cake around. LOGAN opens the letter.

JAMIE: *(To ROBERTA.)* Who made this, you or Claire?

ROBERTA: I did.

JAMIE: Should be edible, then.

             CLAIRE makes a face at JAMIE and sits.

LOGAN: This is dated July fourteenth. Is everyone ready? Here goes. *(Reads.)* Dear Mother and Father, Jamie, Chickadee, Aloysius. I got your parcel today—

ROBERTA: Oh, did he. At last!

LOGAN: *(Reading.)* —along with one from the church. I was glad of both. From the church I got a shirt, a handkerchief, fifty cigarettes, two pair socks and gum. I fared pretty well. The things Mother sent are dandy, especially the underwear. A big thanks to Claire for the fudge. We lobbed it across the line at Fritz. You should have heard him howl!

    JAMIE laughs. He breaks into an imitation of a terrified German soldier.

JAMIE: Gott im Himmel, not ze fudge!

CLAIRE: No one's laughing, Jamie.

LOGAN: *(Reading.)* Father, one of the horses here reminds me of old Fuss. Not that she's a sorrel, but she's as stubborn and bold. *(To ANNA.)* He's always loved horses, has William.

ROBERTA: Ever since he was four.

LOGAN: So they made him a driver. He goes back and forth with supplies. Are you all right with this?

ANNA: *(Although she's not.)* Fine.

LOGAN: *(Resumes reading.)* I love her to pieces. Not the others. They've sworn they'll do her in some dark and moonless night. Her name is Peg, but they call her Pig. She ain't no lady, it's true. If you happen to pass with a pail of water, she'll jam her head in right up to the eyes. And it's a long— *(Catches himself.)* —blankety-blank—walk—

JAMIE: Just read it.

LOGAN: *(Resumes.)* —back to the well. She'll slam her
            nosebag down on the head of anyone walking by,
            to get a good mouthful of oats.

            JAMIE laughs again.

            You should hear the language! You got to forgive
            her, though. She'll go through anything— ditches
            or wire entanglements—and never think to balk.

ANNA: What does he mean? They say everything by saying
            nothing. They're all the same.

LOGAN: Almost done. *(Resumes.)* Been quiet lately. Don't
            worry about me at all. Hope you get that crop off.
            That's it for now. Oh, I made a trip over to Geordie's
            grave. *(Struggles.)* It's near some trees on a bit of a
            rise and set out very nice. Love to all of you. Will.
            P.S. Tell Jamie to quit his whining. Forget about
            joining up. We'll lick the Hun without him. I'll
            box his ears if he doesn't do as he's told. *(Folds the
            letter.)*

JAMIE: *(To ROBERTA.)* I'll bet you asked him to say that.

ROBERTA: I certainly did not.

JAMIE: Well, you told him I'd been whining. When he
            signed up, you said—

LOGAN: Never mind about that. I've told you, we need you
            here.

JAMIE: I didn't choose to be the youngest. Why should I be
            stuck here—

ANNA: I wish I'd crippled all of them, the minute it started.
            The minute! Shot them in the knee or smashed an
            ankle—

ROBERTA: Anna!

ANNA: Or cut off their trigger fingers. Something simple
            like that.

LOGAN: You're dreaming, I'm afraid.

ANNA: No, I was dreaming then. I don't know what I thought. That it would always be some other mother's son who went off to be shot for me?

ROBERTA begins to gather up the dishes.

LOGAN: Let's talk about something cheerful.

ANNA: You sound like C.L. He won't hear a word about it. Not anymore. And if I mention Alexander, he gets up and leaves the room. He says I mustn't dwell on it—

ROBERTA: He's absolutely right.

ANNA: But I can't not dwell on it! I can't fill my days with— silly pink teas and—concerts for French orphans and—whatever they think of next! I can't roll another bandage or pack another Red Cross parcel. And nothing on God's green earth can make me knit another pair of socks! I can't bear the thought of it. Why? So some poor boy can wear them while he's blasted to smithereens?

A silence.

Oh dear. I've worn out my welcome, haven't I? And I've just arrived.

LOGAN: Of course you haven't.

CLAIRE: You couldn't.

ROBERTA: Only I don't know what you'll do with yourself on Thursday afternoon. It's my turn to have them, you see. The Standfast Needle Battalion. That's what Logan calls us. We're having a knitting bee—and it's bound to be socks.

Pause.

ANNA: I'm sorry. I really am sorry. I didn't intend to say that. I meant to behave myself. *(Stands.)* I think I'll go for a walk. Leave the dishes, Roberta.

ROBERTA: Oh no, Claire can—

ANNA: *(Turning on her.)* Promise me you'll leave them!

ROBERTA: *(Taken aback.)* All right! Jamie will fill the wood box for you. Don't give all the scraps to the dog. We're doing our best to fatten the pig. His days are numbered now.

> ANNA exits. CLAIRE stands, moves to the door and stares after her.

JAMIE: That was treason.

CLAIRE: Jamie!

JAMIE: Give 'em the vote and look how they talk.

CLAIRE: She's out of sorts, that's all.

ALOYSIUS: *(Recites.)* The air is full of farewells to the dying,/ And mournings for the dead;/ The heart of Rachel for her children crying,/ Will not be comforted! *(Stands.)* Thank you for supper, Mrs. Reid.

ROBERTA: Are you leaving, too? You've barely touched your cake.

ALOYSIUS: I've had sufficient, Ma'am.

ROBERTA: You haven't even had your tea. Oh, go, Aloysius. Go.

> CLAIRE takes ALOYSIUS's hat from a peg and hands it to him. He puts it on and exits.

CLAIRE: *(To LOGAN.)* I'd like to come with you. May I?

LOGAN: Don't see why not.

CLAIRE: I'll pick some flowers to take. *(Exits.)*

LOGAN: *(To JAMIE.)* Hitch the buggy.

JAMIE: I still say it's treason.

LOGAN: All right.

                 JAMIE exits. LOGAN glances at ROBERTA.

                 She's worn out from the trip.

ROBERTA: She needs to learn some self-restraint. She needs to stiffen her spine.

LOGAN: It's the lack of information. She's fired off letters to everyone she can think of—

ROBERTA: And how is that going to help?

LOGAN: *(Sighs.)* It's only been a few months, Pet.

ROBERTA: Oh, I know. *(Turns away.)* I know.

                 He reaches out and takes her hand. She nods, still turned away.

Scene Two

                 The kitchen, a few hours later. Dusk. In the distance, a hawk is heard: scree! scree! scree! BOHDAN sits in the shadows, a still dark figure in civilian clothes. ANNA enters, with a camera hanging from one shoulder and her arms full of bones. She dumps them on the table, lights a lamp and begins to photograph the bones. Suddenly, she senses a presence and turns.

ANNA: Oh! I thought the house was empty. What are you doing here?

BOHDAN: That's my question.

ANNA: Why?

BOHDAN: I grew up half a mile from here and I've never seen you before.

ANNA: I'm Mr. Reid's sister.

BOHDAN: Are you. I didn't know he had one.

ANNA: Well, he does.

BOHDAN: What's that you dumped on the table?

ANNA: Bones. I found them in the coulee.

BOHDAN: Ah. You've been trespassing then. The coulee belongs to my father.

ANNA: I believe you're mistaken.

BOHDAN: I'm not.

ANNA: But my brother owns the pasture that runs down into it.

BOHDAN: That's right, he owns that end. He sold the rest to my father. Years ago.

ANNA: (*Beat.*) In that case, I am in the wrong. I owe your father an apology.

BOHDAN: He won't accept it.

ANNA: Excuse me?

BOHDAN: He'll want to punish you. He may have come here penniless, but he didn't come here poor; he brought his traditions with him. I don't know what he'd do to you, but I can tell you this: you wouldn't trespass again.

             ANNA laughs, a little uncomfortably.

             You think I'm joking.

ANNA: Aren't you?

BOHDAN: Am I?

ANNA: You have to be. All I've done, for pity's sake, is pick up a few old bones. What would you like me to do, put them back?

BOHDAN: I'd like to know how you found it. No one knew it was there. People rode right by it, never saw it.

ANNA: What are you talking about?

BOHDAN: The buffalo jump. You don't know what it is, do you? Thousands of them died there. Wave after wave, driven over. Now you come along and poke through the bones. Like you had a right.

ANNA: *(Beat.)* I don't believe you've introduced yourself.

BOHDAN: *(Removes his cap.)* Bohdan Stefaniuk.

ANNA: Bohdan. I'm Mrs. McGrath. Tell me the truth now, please. You were teasing, weren't you? Your father wouldn't really—

BOHDAN: Oh, I don't know about that. He's Ukrainian, after all. Barely civilized. That's what you people think, isn't it?

ANNA: Is it?

BOHDAN: Pretty much. *(Stands.)* It's pretty much what I heard, growing up. That and a whole lot worse.

             He moves to the table and begins to arrange the bones into piles.

             You've got quite a collection. What do you want with them?

ANNA: I really can't answer that.

BOHDAN: *(Holds a bone to the light.)* Did you find any arrowheads?

ANNA: Yes, I found a beauty. *(Takes it from a pocket.)* It belongs to your father, I guess.

BOHDAN: My father won't miss one arrowhead. The coulee is littered with them. But you ought to put it back.

ANNA: Why?

BOHDAN: It was blessed before it was used. It's a holy thing. So the Indians tell me.

ANNA: And what do you think?

BOHDAN: I think— *(Two beats.)* —that life of any kind is sacred, and the taking of it—is also a sacred thing. It should be done with reverence. Pity. Awe. Only when strictly necessary. If at all.

ANNA: So that's why you haven't joined up.

BOHDAN stiffens.

I'm not going to hand you a feather—or dust you with talcum powder. I wish there were more like you. What are you staring at?

BOHDAN: I took you for English.

ANNA: Which means?

BOHDAN: English women don't talk like that.

ANNA: That's why the world's in the mess it's in.

BOHDAN: Because of English women? Is that what it is! Nothing to do with the Hun at all.

ANNA: *(Quietly, ferociously.)* Don't patronize me.

He turns to her in surprise.

I lost my son over there. I don't know how it happened, not even the time of day. But I know why he was there. He was there because his elders—I don't exclude myself!—allowed themselves to believe it was a holy crusade. Some of those elders were women. Mostly English women. Pretending to be high-minded when they were really out for blood. If I choose to blame them—or anyone else who comes to mind—believe me I damn well will!

She begins piling dishes, noisily, into a basin. In the distance, a fiddle is heard, playing a mournful tune.

BOHDAN: I didn't mean to offend you.

ANNA: No.

BOHDAN: You caught me off guard. *(Beat.)* I'm sorry about your son.

ANNA: Yes.

BOHDAN: *(With a gesture towards the bones.)* Is that why you've dug these up?

ANNA: No, of course not. Good heavens. I'm a little crazy, but I'm not completely crazy. Not yet, anyway.

She smiles; she has an arresting smile. He turns away.

BOHDAN: I've sorted them for you, as you can see. Maybe I didn't need to. Maybe you know how it's done.

ANNA: *(Moves close enough to look.)* No, I don't, in fact.

BOHDAN: Neither do I. I'm only trying to impress you.

ANNA: You mean they're not sorted at all?

BOHDAN: *(With a shrug.)* Into piles.

ANNA: *(Laughs.)* You're a professional, aren't you? An expert tease.

BOHDAN: No, I'm an amateur. I do like to make people laugh. Especially women. Especially beautiful women.

ANNA moves away. She picks up the kettle.

Now I've embarrassed you.

ANNA: *(Pours water in a basin.)* You haven't said why you're here.

BOHDAN: And suddenly she's afraid.

ANNA: Nonsense. Answer the question.

BOHDAN: Mr. Reid wanted to see me.

ANNA: Well, he was called away.

BOHDAN: I gathered. Will he be late?

ANNA: I expect so. *(Quickly.)* Then again, maybe not.

BOHDAN: You are afraid. I knew it. You shouldn't be. Even if I meant to harm you, you'd only have to yell. Aloysius would come to your rescue, like the good old sweat he is. He's just down in the bunkhouse. So there's nothing to worry about.

ANNA: I'm not the least bit worried.

BOHDAN: Besides, I don't blame you, you know. You come back from raiding our coulee—to find a stranger here. A Galician, to boot. That's the name for it, right? Anyone who had the misfortune not to be born a Brit?

ANNA: You really don't like us, do you?

BOHDAN: I make the odd exception.

ANNA: Well, I'm glad to hear that!

BOHDAN: Your brother, for instance, I like very much.

ANNA: My brother is a gem.

BOHDAN: He has integrity. And quite a stunning — sister.

ANNA: Bohdan. *(Faces him.)* Are you flirting with me? Because if you are, I think you should know—

BOHDAN: Your hair is as black as a crow's wing. How did an English woman come by hair like that?

ANNA: That's a very impertinent question.

BOHDAN: I know.

> *JAMIE suddenly enters, with newspapers.*

JAMIE: Aunt Anna? Who are you—? *(Sees BOHDAN.)* Oh.

ANNA: Jamie, you must know—

JAMIE: Sure. *(Flustered.)* I mean—well, in a way. *(To BOHDAN.)* Father had to leave. I'm sorry.

BOHDAN: To nicho. [It's nothing.] I'll be back.

ANNA: *(To JAMIE.)* I thought you'd gone with them.

JAMIE: I stayed to read the papers. Strictly against the law. *(Sets the papers down.)* My father thinks he's the only one who can stand to know the facts. *(To BOHDAN.)* Looks like a big push coming, if you read between the lines. William might get to be in it.

ANNA: God forbid.

JAMIE: I only hope there's still work to do when I get over there. They all say it won't last long, now that the Yanks are in. *(To BOHDAN, shyly.)* Do you think they're right?

BOHDAN: I'd be the last one to know. *(Starts off.)*

ANNA: *(To BOHDAN.)* I may want to dig again.

BOHDAN: *(Turns back.)* Why?

ANNA: Will your father object or not?

BOHDAN: My father is the softest man you'd ever care to meet. He'd dig them for you himself if he thought you needed them. I'm of a different mind. I think you should leave them alone.

ANNA: Why?

BOHDAN: Just a feeling.

ANNA: A superstition.

BOHDAN: Considering how they got there. Mrs. McGrath. Jamie.

> *He puts on his cap and exits. ANNA shudders.*

ANNA: What an uncomfortable man!

JAMIE: *(Meaning the bones.)* You'd better get these out of here.

ANNA: *(Turns to him.)* Jamie.

JAMIE: Mother will go through the roof.

ANNA: Forget about going over. Put it out of your mind. This family has given enough already. It's time we thought of ourselves.

JAMIE: There she goes! The queen of treason.

> *JAMIE sits and tries to shut her out by reading a newspaper.*

ANNA: Be glad you're not there already. Be glad you're only fifteen. And for God's sake stop dreaming about it. It's just an illusion.

JAMIE: A what?!

ANNA: You heard me.

JAMIE: You don't believe in anything.

ANNA: *(Beat.)* I believe that boys who hang around kitchens when there are dishes to be done should expect to be tossed a towel.

> *She tosses him a towel.*

JAMIE: I know about you. You got kicked out of the church—

ANNA: *(Begins to wash dishes.)* You're damned right I did.

JAMIE: For fighting with the minister. You threw a rack of hymnals at him—

ANNA: Two. I let him have it.

JAMIE: They had to drag you out of there.

ANNA: Do you know what that great oaf said? That any man who couldn't be useful to his country was really better off dead.

JAMIE: He's right.

ANNA: *(Stops washing.)* He signed up the moment he could—your cousin Alexander. The day he turned seventeen. Came through the door looking pleased as punch. *I've given myself a birthday present. Please be happy for me!* A boy who'd hardly even held a gun.

JAMIE: Grandfather was a soldier—

ANNA: Yes, and he died as one.

JAMIE: Try being proud of that!

He throws down the towel and exits.

Scene Three

The farmyard. The following morning. CLAIRE stands at a wooden trestle, plucking a chicken. On the ground is a tub of water. ANNA enters, her camera hanging from her shoulder, carrying a kettle of boiling water, which she pours in the tub. CLAIRE wipes her brow with the back of one feather-covered hand. We hear chickens squawking, off.

CLAIRE: I loathe this job!

ANNA: Then let me do it.

CLAIRE: (*Shakes her head.*) It's penance.

             ROBERTA enters, with a headless chicken.

             Isn't it, Mother? (*Brandishes the chicken.*) Penance.

ROBERTA: I'd trade you any day. (*To ANNA.*) Geordie and
             Will used to do this for me. The circus, they called
             it. (*To CLARE.*) Remember? Half a dozen headless
             chickens, tearing around in circles, until they all fell
             down.

             ANNA snaps ROBERTA's photograph.

             Anna!

ANNA: (*Reaches for the chicken.*) I'll do that one for you.

ROBERTA: Sure?

ANNA: To keep her company.

             *ROBERTA hands the chicken to ANNA, then picks
             up the kettle.*

ROBERTA: Thank God the weather held. They'll get the last of
             the wheat cut, with a little luck, this morning. Well,
             I'll leave you to it.

             *ROBERTA rushes off. ANNA plunges the chicken
             into the boiling water and begins to pluck.*

ANNA: There were wild flowers in my room last night. Are
             you the one to thank?

CLAIRE: (*Flashes her a smile.*) Mother calls them weeds. They
             grow like blazes in the pastures. Is there anything
             else you need?

ANNA: Just a good night's sleep.

CLAIRE: I poked through your closet. I hope you don't

mind. You have such lovely things. There's a dress
I'd give my eyeteeth for.

ANNA: Is there. Which one?

CLAIRE: The one with the emerald collar.

ANNA: It's yours! I'll make it over for you.

CLAIRE: That's not what I meant at all.

ANNA: I know, but I'd like to do it. I hate that dress on me.
           I hate myself in all my clothes. I hate seeing myself
           in the mirror!

CLAIRE: It's too much trouble.

ANNA: No, it's not. Your mother's got that brand new
           Raymond. I'd like to try it out. Then you'll have
           something new to wear when all the boys come
           calling.

CLAIRE: All the boys! This isn't the city, Aunt Anna. The
           ones I liked are gone and as for the ones who
           aren't—I couldn't go out with them. I'd feel like a
           traitor. However…

ANNA: Yes?

CLAIRE: I am seeing someone Friday night. Don't mention
           it in front of Mother. She doesn't like him much.

ANNA: Ah. You like him, though.

CLAIRE: I like that Mother doesn't like him.

ANNA: I see. One of those!

           They exchange a smile. ANNA turns away.

           Tempting, but strictly off-limits.

CLAIRE: Well, not entirely off-limits—

ANNA: *(To herself.)* Dangerous, too.

CLAIRE gives her a curious glance.

That type. They throw you off-kilter. Has this fellow done that to you?

CLAIRE: A bit.

ANNA: Is he the reason you didn't answer?

CLAIRE: *(Shakes her head.)* I didn't know how to explain. It was so good of you to invite me. But I'd have worried, and that would have spoiled it.

ANNA: About your mother, you mean?

CLAIRE: She's always been a worker, but it's different now. She works as though work will save her. But it's Father I'm most concerned about. He seems so frail to me.

ANNA: He's always been thin as a twig.

CLAIRE: I don't mean that kind of frail. He — *(Breaks off; reconsiders.)* He was so close to Geordie. Sometimes I wondered why. That Geordie! Always squabbling with some one, right from the day he was born. I used to get fed up with it. Now I'm sorry I did. *(Beat.)* He left a mess in Standfast.

ANNA: What do you mean?

CLAIRE: Two girls half mad for him. I don't know what he promised them, but they both act like widows now. Father is mortified. Either one might have had his child. *(Glances at ANNA.)* Do you find that shocking?

ANNA: No.

CLAIRE: I would have, once. Things are different now. When you fall in love with a soldier, it's hard to hold anything back.

ANNA: Is that the voice of experience?

CLAIRE: I'm quoting Sarah. She and Art were high school sweethearts. When he signed up, she made a decision. Now he's back with no legs. I wonder if she regrets it. I wonder what I'd have done. Or what I'd do now, if I fell in love. The men are giving— have given—so much. And there's so little we can do. It's all a bit confusing.

ANNA: Be careful, my love. Don't give your heart to anyone before you know yourself. All your life you'll wonder—what else might have been. We get locked in so soon. Somebody's wife, somebody's mother. That's all very well. But what we might have been and done—that's what comes back to haunt us, in the dead of night. You should live on your own for a while. Pick a city; I'll send you. New York would be wonderful. Rent a room and study art! God know, the world needs painters.

CLAIRE: I couldn't let you do that.

ANNA: I can't imagine a better way to spend your uncle's money. Really, I wish you would. Your mother can manage on her own, once the harvest's in.

CLAIRE: It isn't that. They need me. And I know I need them. Now that Geordie— *(Breaks off.)* And with William. I wouldn't enjoy myself.

ANNA: Think about it, at least.

CLAIRE: *(Uncertainly.)* All right.

ANNA: Unless you fall in love, of course. Maybe you already have.

CLAIRE: *(With her eyes averted.)* I hardly know him.

ANNA: But you're excited. Where is he taking you?

CLAIRE: To a dance.

ANNA: If you try on that dress after supper tonight and we get you measured up, I'll have it ready for Friday night. Every man in the place will be drooling over you.

CLAIRE: Wonderful! I want to look stunning for him. I want to look better than I've ever looked. I want Mother pacing all evening!

CLAIRE and ANNA exit, with the chickens.

Scene Four

The verandah. Several days later. Early Friday evening. Clouds are gathering; the wind is on the rise. In the background CLAIRE is singing: a World War I standard. ANNA and LOGAN are talking while he mends a trace and she takes bones from a basket and arranges them on the verandah. She has her camera with her.

LOGAN: Disappointed? Think about what I left. A life spent slaving for someone else. I'd have hated that.

A gunshot shatters the evening quiet. ANNA starts.

Besides. If you'd seen the prairies when I first saw them—I'll tell you what. They were so goddamned beautiful, they took your breath away. Do you know that when I first came west, there were flowers everywhere? Far as the eye could see. Bluebells and orange lilies and wild roses—pink and white and red.

Another gunshot.

As though a vast oriental carpet had been cast down across the plain. I walked on flowers, I slept on flowers. I felt like a young giant.

ROBERTA appears like a shadow at the screened door.

I remember wandering out one morning, the first year I was here, to pick mushrooms after a rain. And one of them, I swear to God, was twenty-one inches around. Thought I'd found paradise.

ROBERTA: (*Very dry.*) And then came winter.

> *ROBERTA opens the screened door and steps out onto the verandah, wiping her hands on her apron. LOGAN glances at her.*

LOGAN: Shouldn't have got started.

ROBERTA: Why did you, then?

LOGAN: Why? I'm a daft old bunny-lugs, that's why.

ANNA: Bunny-lugs! What an expression. I haven't heard it in years.

LOGAN: Haven't used it in years. See what happens when you get me talking? No telling what will emerge.

> *ANNA snaps a photograph of the bones.*

ROBERTA: (*To ANNA.*) What on earth are you doing?

ANNA: I can't get them out of my head.

> *Gunshot.*

ROBERTA: Merciful heavens!

ANNA: What *is* that?

> *Gunshot.*

ROBERTA: Geordie sent it to him. And a box of souvenirs. Why I'll never know.

LOGAN: (*Checking out the sky.*) He'll soon be out of ammunition.

> *Gunshot. JAMIE groans, off. Another gunshot. JAMIE whoops, off.*

ROBERTA: So you keep telling me.

ANNA: You look worried, Logan. Is it going to rain?

LOGAN: No, it's going to blow over, but I'm worrying anyway. Farmer's prerogative.

              A dog barks, off. We hear a horse-drawn buggy approaching.

ROBERTA: Here he comes now, that fellow of Claire's. *(To LOGAN.)* Should we tell her she can't go?

LOGAN: We can tell her. Will she listen?

ROBERTA: She will if it comes from you.

LOGAN: *(Sighs.)* She's nineteen, Roberta.

ROBERTA: And he's even older than William. And just back. God only knows what he's been up to, all those months over there.

LOGAN: Like fighting, is that what you mean? Putting his neck on the line?

ROBERTA: Go ahead and mock me. You know what I'm talking about.

              The buggy comes to a stop, off.

BOHDAN: *(Off.)* What have you got there?

JAMIE: *(Off.)* Geordie took it off a Hun.

              The screened door opens and CLAIRE appears, in a dress with a emerald collar. She assumes a pose.

CLAIRE: Well? How do I look?

ANNA: Ravishing!

BOHDAN: *(Off.)* A turnip-grip Mauser. Nice.

JAMIE: *(Off.)* He sent a whole box of things.

ANNA focuses her camera on CLAIRE.

CLAIRE:　　Papa-Mine?

LOGAN:　　Nearly as pretty as your mother.

JAMIE:　　*(Off.)* I have to keep it stashed in the barn.

ANNA snaps a photograph.

CLAIRE:　　Mother? What do you think?

ROBERTA:　　*(Precisely.)* I think you look very nice. However—

CLAIRE:　　I love it, Aunt Annie. *(Kisses ANNA.)* Thank you.

ROBERTA:　　Now listen, dear—

> *She breaks off as BOHDAN and JAMIE enter from the yard. BOHDAN hands JAMIE the pistol. CLAIRE runs down the steps. ANNA turns abruptly away.*

BOHDAN:　　*(To CLAIRE.)* I'm a little late. I'm sorry.

CLAIRE:　　You're right on time. *(Turns to the others.)* Won't anyone say hello?

LOGAN:　　Of course we will. *(Stands; offers his hand.)* Bohdan.

BOHDAN:　　*(Shakes his hand.)* Mr. Reid.

LOGAN:　　Sorry I missed you the other night. What I meant to offer is this. Sixty cents a day, plus room and board. Not as rich as the army, but—

BOHDAN:　　When do I start?

LOGAN:　　Tomorrow, if you can. I'll get you to deal with the pig. Jamie can help you scald it. After that, we'll see. I can use you until the harvest's in.

BOHDAN:　　Suits me.

LOGAN:　　Well! That's settled, then.

CLAIRE: *(To BOHDAN.)* You remember my mother.

BOHDAN: Mrs. Reid.

               ROBERTA barely acknowledges BOHDAN.

CLAIRE: I want you to meet my aunt.

               CLAIRE leads BOHDAN to ANNA, who stands immobilized.

               Aunt Anna, this is Bohdan. Mrs. McGrath.

               No response.

LOGAN: Anna?

ANNA: I'm sorry, I'm—so sorry! *(To BOHDAN.)* It's nice to see you again.

CLAIRE: *(Glances at BOHDAN.)* Again?

ANNA: Bohdan! What a strong name. I like the sound of it. C.L., my husband—Claire's uncle—has a strong one, too. Actually, it's Coeur de Lion. Heart of a lion, you see. His mother was French and an optimist. That's what he always says. He finds the name embarrassing. Prefers the initials.

BOHDAN: I see.

ANNA: We named our boy Alexander. Also very strong. I thought it would protect him, but— *(Breaks off.)*

               A brief silence.

CLAIRE: We'd better be going.

ROBERTA: What time will you be home?

CLAIRE: The dance is over at midnight. *(Starts off, leading BOHDAN.)*

LOGAN: *(To BOHDAN.)* You'll leave with the others?

BOHDAN: Yes, sir. Good night.

ROBERTA: Twelve-thirty, then?

LOGAN: Good night.

ROBERTA: Claire?

> *CLAIRE and BOHDAN manage to exit without making a commitment.*

Honestly, that girl. And now he's going to live here!

LOGAN: We need the help.

ROBERTA: I know, but I don't like it. There's a chip on his shoulder the size of Gibraltar.

LOGAN: He's a goddamned paragon of courage. What more do you want?

BOHDAN: *(Off.)* Giddup.

> *We hear the buggy move away. LOGAN turns to JAMIE.*

LOGAN: Put that away for a while.

JAMIE: What do you mean, a while?

LOGAN: Until further notice.

JAMIE: Why? It's mine to use if I want to.

LOGAN: Don't argue with me. *(Starts off.)*

ROBERTA: *(To LOGAN.)* Where are you off to now? You're not going to tinker with that tractor.

LOGAN: I'm feeling lucky tonight.

JAMIE: *(To LOGAN.)* Even for gophers?

LOGAN: *(Over his shoulder.)* You heard me.

> *LOGAN exits. JAMIE shouts after him.*

JAMIE: You could at least tell me why!

ROBERTA: *(To JAMIE.)* Watch your mouth.

JAMIE: Well! *(Shoots ANNA a murderous glance.)* It didn't matter a week ago.

ROBERTA: Take it back to the barn.

JAMIE exits. ANNA stares after BOHDAN.

ANNA: Who is he?—that man.

ROBERTA: He's trouble, that's who he is.

ANNA: A paragon of courage?

ROBERTA: He was decorated. *(Grudgingly.)* Twice. And wounded, apparently. You wouldn't know it to look at him.

ANNA: He hides it pretty well. But it's there all the same. You can't help but feel it—like a cold draft in a warm room.

ROBERTA: *(Facing her.)* What are you talking about?

ANNA: He's not hard to look at, is he?

ROBERTA: He's nothing but a sleazy bohunk. She's only seeing him to annoy me. She doesn't think I know that, but I do. *(Opens the screened door.)* I was nineteen once myself. I had a mother, too.

> *ROBERTA exits. The silence is broken by the off-stage sound of an engine trying to start: swish swish swish swish swish swish bang bang. ANNA covers her ears. A much louder bang.*

LOGAN: *(A long way off.)* Sufferin' Sam Hill—!

A final bang, then silence.

Scene Five

> *The verandah. Very early the following morning.*
> *A night of wind and stars. In the distance, a coyote*
> *howls. CLAIRE sits on the verandah, deep in*
> *shadow. A fiddle is heard, off, playing a mournful*
> *tune. The screened door opens and ANNA steps*
> *out.*

ANNA: I heard the buggy come and go, but I didn't hear you come up.

CLAIRE: Weren't you able to sleep?

ANNA: Aloysius isn't sleeping either. Makes me shiver, that tune.

CLAIRE: He could make a jig sound mournful. If he knew a jig. *(Meaning the bones.)* Does Mother know these are here?

ANNA: She's indulging me, for the moment.

> *ANNA lights a cigarette. CLAIRE looks at her in*
> *surprise.*

Do you disapprove?

CLAIRE: *(Although she does.)* Don't be silly.

ANNA: I'm told it's not ladylike. All the more reason, I say. How was the dance?

CLAIRE: I enjoyed it.

ANNA: He's a good dancer?

CLAIRE: He is.

ANNA: He liked the dress?

CLAIRE: Very much.

ANNA: Does he frighten you?

CLAIRE: What a question!

ANNA: He frightens me.

CLAIRE: *(Hesitates.)* I've never gone out with a soldier before.
             A real one, I mean. I don't know what I expected,
             but— *(Breaks off.)*

ANNA: But what?

CLAIRE: I thought he'd talk about it. He refuses to. Except
             now and then in jest. As though it were an
             enormous joke. He's like that about a lot of things.
             Things that matter to me. Faith, for instance.
             Prayer. He says God is sound asleep, so what's the
             use of prayer?

ANNA: He's right.

CLAIRE: You don't mean that.

ANNA: Is he kind to you?

CLAIRE: He is, but— *(Breaks off.)* I don't know. I think he'd
             rather look at me than listen to me. I'm not sure how
             I feel about that.

             *ROBERTA appears at the screened door. CLAIRE
             and ANNA retreat into the shadows. The door opens
             and ROBERTA steps out.*

ROBERTA: Aloysius! Aloysius! We could use some sleep up
             here!

             The music stops abruptly.

             (To herself.) Hasn't learned a new tune since 1865!

             ROBERTA disappears inside. Beat.

ANNA: It's nice to be looked at, though. To really be seen. I
             find it irresistible. Don't you?

CLAIRE: *(Embarrassed.)* I don't know how to answer that.

ANNA: *(With a glance at the sky.)* Your father's hunch was right. He said it would blow over.

CLAIRE: He has a nose for things. It's uncanny at times.

ANNA: It runs in the family. In the village she came from, our mother was known as fey.

CLAIRE: An odd word, isn't it?

ANNA: You've probably heard the stories.

CLAIRE: I know she saw my grandfather's ghost.

ANNA: I'll never forget that night.

CLAIRE: Tell me.

ANNA: She woke us in the early hours and announced that our father was dead. He'd come to her in his uniform—scarlet tunic, the works!—all the way from South Africa. Stood right next to her bed. I prayed for once she'd be wrong. I might have saved my breath. There were so many other things. She'd know a letter was on its way before it was even written. She could always find what you'd lost. She could find what half the village lost! Nothing was ever a mystery, not with her around. She'd get to the bottom of things.

CLAIRE: Because she could.

ANNA: Because she had to. *(Turns to stare off.)* Does he bunk in with Aloysius?

CLAIRE: *(Glances at her.)* It sleeps four, in a pinch.

ANNA: I wonder what they talk about, in the dark of night. Women, I suppose.

CLAIRE: Not Aloysius.

ANNA: You never know.

CLAIRE: I can't imagine it.

ANNA: I was a little sweet on him once.

CLAIRE: Aloysius!

ANNA: When I first came west. I think in my heart of hearts I've always liked the strays.

                A curious look from CLAIRE.

                What's the matter?

CLAIRE: *(Looks away.)* Nothing, just— *(Catches herself.)* —wondering. Whether you're fey, as well.

ANNA: Not like Mother...

CLAIRE: But?

ANNA: *(Beat.)* Alexander. I was cleaning his room one morning, not long after he'd left. There was a shaft of sunlight on the floor and dust drifting up from that. I watched the dust float upwards and suddenly I knew. I felt it— *(Lays a hand on her stomach.)* —here. I sat down right away and wrote to him. I wrote about everything. All the years that lay ahead. All the things he'd do. How much I'd learned from him.

CLAIRE: I'm sure that's one letter he treasured.

ANNA: *(Turns away.)* I didn't mail it.

CLAIRE: Why not?

ANNA: He'd have known what inspired it. I'm sure he'd have known.

                Brief silence. Both stare off.

                I keep reading his letters. They're like a puzzle to me. Exquisitely written. Evocative. Maddeningly vague! Full of a kind of—wonder. That he never explains. It's there in the details, in the odd little turn of phrase. A hint—just a hint of something,

something…that I like to think gave him solace. I hope to God it did. Maybe it would for me, as well, if I only—if— *(Breaks off; faces her.)* I'd like to talk to Bohdan.

CLAIRE: Well, he'll be around. *(Beat.)* Oh. You mean about— *(Breaks off.)* But I've just finished saying—I've told you—he won't talk about that.

ANNA: There's got to be a way around it.

CLAIRE: Like what?

ANNA: Persuasion.

> *ROBERTA appears like a shadow at the screened door.*

He can help me, Claire.

CLAIRE: I don't see how.

ANNA: He can. He was there.

ROBERTA: *(Overlapping.)* Claire?

CLAIRE: Yes, Mother!

ROBERTA: *(Offended.)* There's no need to answer like that. What are you doing?

CLAIRE: Talking.

ROBERTA: What about?

ANNA: Just talking.

ROBERTA: But it's nearly two o'clock!

ANNA: Goodness. Is it already? *(Moves to the door.)*

ROBERTA: We've a long day ahead of us.

ANNA: That's true. *(Slips through the screened door.)* Thank you. *(To both of them.)* Goodnight.

ROBERTA: Claire?

> *CLAIRE moves to the screened door.*

What's wrong? What did he do to you? Claire!

> *CLAIRE disappears inside. ROBERTA closes the screened door and follows her. The lamp inside is blown out.*

Scene Six

> *Exterior of the smokehouse. The following morning. We hear a rooster crow. ANNA and ROBERTA roll a barrel on. A pig is heard squealing, off.*

BOHDAN: *(Off.)* I'll take the front, you take the back.

JAMIE: *(Off.)* Get him, get him, get him!

> *The pig squeals again. ANNA turns toward the sound.*

ANNA: How do they do it, Roberta?

ROBERTA: Do what? Oh. They hang it by its hind legs. It's best done on a cold day, but we have no choice. We'll need the meat for the threshing crew. If they ever come.

JAMIE: *(Off.)* Grab him!

BOHDAN: *(Off.)* He's on to us!

JAMIE: *(Off.)* Hold on!

> *The pig continues to squeal. CLAIRE enters with hooks. She enters the smokehouse and hangs them on metal rods. ROBERTA takes up a broom and begins to sweep. The louder the pig squeals, the harder she sweeps. ANNA takes up her camera and trains it off-stage, in the direction of the pig.*

ROBERTA: *(To CLAIRE.)* Where's your father?

CLAIRE: Working on the tractor.

ROBERTA: Run and ask him when he wants his dinner.

CLAIRE: What's the point?

BOHDAN: *(Off.)* Twice around with the rope.

CLAIRE: He'll just say noon. He always does.

BOHDAN: *(Off.)* That's it. Good and tight.

ROBERTA: If you think he's that predictable—

                ANNA snaps a photograph of the off-stage action.

                Anna, for heaven's sake!

ANNA: What's wrong?

ROBERTA: If you have to use that thing, can't you use it on something attractive? Why on earth would you photograph that?

ANNA: Because it's hard to look at.

ROBERTA: That's—

ANNA: With the naked eye. But when you take a photograph—

                Suddenly, off-stage, we hear an engine starting: swish swish swish swish swish swish bang bang bang bang. ANNA covers her ears.

ROBERTA: He's determined to get that thing going. It cost a fortune, you know. I told him he might as well stand on the doorstep in a good strong northwest wind and let the money fly, but would he listen?

                The banging goes on and on. The women turn towards the sound.

That sounds promising.

> *She has no sooner spoken than a huge bang is heard, then silence. The women sag with disappointment.*

LOGAN: *(A long way off.)* Goddamn bleedin'—!

ROBERTA: *(Sets the broom aside, starts off.)* Let me know what your father says.

BOHDAN: *(Off.)* I'll hold him steady. You wind it.

ROBERTA: Claire?

CLAIRE: All right, all right, I will!

ROBERTA: Someone's a little tired today. I can't imagine why.

> *ROBERTA hurries off. CLAIRE turns to ANNA, who is watching the action off-stage.*

CLAIRE: Aunt Anna.

ANNA: *(To herself.)* My God…

CLAIRE: I don't want you talking to Bohdan. I'd rather you didn't, I mean. I don't think it's right.

ANNA: *(Faces her.)* My goodness. So protective. I think you're in love with him.

> *The pig squeals again. This time the sound is horrible: the frantic, visceral protest of a creature about to die.*

CLAIRE: You don't know what it's like for him. I do. I saw it last night. I had to fake a headache to get him out of there. He could hardly sit down for a minute without someone approaching him. First a little chitchat, then the burning question: *what's it like over there?* He was pale as a ghost in half an hour. Shaking from head to foot. Do you see what I'm trying to say? You're my aunt, my precious Aunt Anna. You can't be like the rest. You can't be chasing after Bohdan with your burning question. Maybe—

ANNA: Don't you worry about Bohdan. He faced down the Kaiser's army. He has nothing to fear from me.

ANNA exits. CLAIRE exits.

Scene Seven

Exterior of the smoke house, some time later. BOHDAN enters, with buckets containing blood and internal body parts. He sets them down, exits and returns with part of a pig carcass, which he sets on a trestle. He removes his jacket, picks up a knife, hones it. Throughout most of the scene, he will work at cutting up the meat, etc. ANNA enters.

ANNA: You should have told me who you were.

BOHDAN: *(Glances at her.)* Mrs. McGrath.

ANNA: How was I to know? From the way you talked I had to assume— *(Breaks off.)* If you felt that way about killing— *(Breaks off again.)* Why did you go?

BOHDAN: *(Shrugs.)* The usual thing.

ANNA: Which is?

BOHDAN: Couldn't think of another way to get the hell out of Standfast.

ANNA: I've asked you not to patronize me.

BOHDAN: Is that what I'm doing?

ANNA: Yes!

BOHDAN: *(Beat.)* It wasn't the rhetoric, that's for sure. I didn't believe in God, that King of yours has never meant beans to me and as for Country—

ANNA: Exactly.

BOHDAN: I guess I thought what everyone thought—that it
             would be a lark. I couldn't wait to get over there.
             Now are you satisfied?

ANNA: Then why did you say what you said? That life of
             any kind is sacred.

BOHDAN: It is.

ANNA: Yet you went over and took it.

BOHDAN: I did.

ANNA: Is that not a contradiction?

BOHDAN: Tak. [Yes.]

ANNA: You really are the most infuriating man!

BOHDAN: You can always walk away. In fact, maybe you
             should. This won't be pretty.

ANNA: Claire says I mustn't ask you this. What's it like
             over there?

             BOHDAN stiffens.

             Please, Bohdan. I lost my only child. And I don't
             know how. I can't imagine it.

BOHDAN: You should thank your stars for that.

ANNA: But I'll never—I'll never— *(Struggles.)* —I can't
             get over it! I don't know where he's—if he's...in
             a thousand pieces. Buried. I don't know if it was
             night or day. Was it fast or— *(Breaks off.)* I have
             nothing...nothing— *(Breaks off again.)* How do I go
             on?

BOHDAN: *(Several beats.)* I couldn't tell you, even if I wanted
             to.

ANNA: Why not?

BOHDAN: Maybe in Ukrainian. You know it?

ANNA: There's nothing wrong with your English.

BOHDAN: Not my English. English!

ANNA: It's a perfectly good language—

BOHDAN: Nee! [No!]

ANNA: You're making excuses.

BOHDAN: *(Turns on her.)* Watch it, Mrs. McGrath. Lick a knife and you cut your tongue.

ANNA: I'm ready for that.

BOHDAN: No, you're not.

ANNA: You think I'd be shocked. You're wrong. Lies are shocking. Evasions!

BOHDAN: You're a stubborn woman—

ANNA: Save them for Claire. I don't want them.

BOHDAN: And a bossy one. Your husband puts up with that?

ANNA: Soon after he got to France. He said there'd been some *action*. Now there's an ambiguous word! He was sent out to fetch the dead. One of them was a friend. *A white body, splendid under the moon! I lay down beside him.* Why? *The beauty of things awoke again for me.* What was he talking about? How can there be beauty where a friend lies dead? Explain that to me, Bohdan. Bohdan, Bohdan! Such a powerful name. If I were Claire, I'd never stop saying it. *(Moves closer.)* How were you wounded, Bohdan?

            BOHDAN has begun to shake. His actions reflect his anxiety.

BOHDAN: I don't talk about that.

ANNA: Why not?

BOHDAN: Doesn't interest me.

ANNA: You're lying.

BOHDAN: *(A warning.)* Careful.

ANNA: Of course it interests you.

BOHDAN: You're at it again. Trespassing!

ANNA: Look me in the eye and say it. You can't, can you?

BOHDAN: *(Starting to lose it.)* I can, but I don't want to. You're too damn serious. You should smile more often. Smile through your tears, like the song says. You have a smile a man likes to see. Use it once in a while. Loosen up, goddamnit. Do a little flirting.

ANNA: What's flirting got to do with it?

BOHDAN: *(Points at his temple.)* Dumai, dumai! [Think, think!] You'll figure it out.

ANNA: *(Abruptly.)* Where is your mother, Bohdan?

BOHDAN: I don't talk about her.

ANNA: The reason I'm asking—

BOHDAN: Ever.

ANNA: All right, but here's what I think. One way or another, she's absent. And that's a terrible shame. Because now is when you really need her.

BOHDAN: You don't know what I need.

ANNA: I know what you think you need. I can't give you that. I can only give you what your mother would have given. Pity, Bohdan! I can be shameless when it comes to soldiers, when it comes to pity. I can be bottomless.

He glances at her.

We can help each other. You have something you need to say.

BOHDAN: Yob tvoyou mat! [Fuck your mother!] You don't let up, do you?

ANNA: Something happened to you. Tell me about it! Please.

BOHDAN: *(Losing it.)* 'Smatter with you, for chrissake?

> *He suddenly throws down the knife. He shoves his hand in one of the buckets; it comes up dripping with blood. He smears it on a wall.*

Here! Here! Here!

> *He dips his hand in the pail again and paints his face with blood.*

ANNA: What are you doing? Stop it! *(Grabs his hand.)* Get hold of yourself!

> *He pulls his hand away, dips it again in the bucket, grasps her and paints her face with blood.*

Don't!

> *He continues to dab blood on her face, her throat, her arms.*

BOHDAN: In your hair. Up your nose. In your mouth.

ANNA: Stop it! For God's sake—

> *He empties the bucket on her skirt and shoes, drops the bucket, wheels around, grabs a handful of intestines or organs from the other bucket, intending to throw them at her. He manages to stop himself.*

BOHDAN: Now do you—now? Durna! [Crazy woman!]

He backs away. He has begun to wheeze.

You asked for that, you stubborn, stubborn—! You asked for that!

He staggers into the shadows, struggling to get his breath. She backs away from the entrails—shaking, sickened, gagging. She begins to make unintelligible sounds of revulsion. JAMIE enters, with buckets of water. He stops abruptly.

JAMIE: My God!

ANNA: I just—I just—! It's nobody's business, you hear? I slipped, that's all, I— *(Breaks off.)* It's private, Jamie, understand? Off you go, then.

JAMIE: But—

ANNA: Go!

JAMIE sets down the buckets and exits. ANNA removes her blouse. BOHDAN steps out of the shadows, kneels by the water buckets, takes her hand and begins to wash the blood from her body.

End of Act I.

Act II

Scene One

The kitchen, that evening. Suppertime. LOGAN, ROBERTA, CLAIRE, JAMIE, ALOYSIUS and BOHDAN stand at the table.

ALL BUT BOHDAN: *(Sing.)* Be present at our table, Lord. / Be everywhere adored; / Bless these thy gifts, and grant that we / May with our lives thank thee.

ROBERTA: Amen.

Everyone sits.

LOGAN: *(To CLAIRE.)* Very nice, Chickadee.

ROBERTA: *(To BOHDAN, passing a platter.)* Here you are. You start.

BOHDAN takes the platter.

There's plenty more of everything. Jamie, pass things along. *(No response.)* Jamie!

JAMIE passes a bowl.

They're both in a daze. *(To LOGAN.)* You must have worked them too hard. At this rate, once the threshing starts they'll be fast asleep at the table!

LOGAN: They got the pig slaughtered and cut and hung. And put in a long afternoon.

ANNA enters.

ROBERTA: *(To ANNA.)* We had to start. I'm sorry.

ANNA: *(Sitting.)* Quite all right. *(Meets LOGAN's eyes.)* A little peaky.

JAMIE: I'll bet.

ANNA throws JAMIE a warning glance.

A lazy liver will do that. Or a deranged digestive system. Which is it, Aunt Anna?

ANNA: *(In confusion.)* I—

JAMIE: Either way. What you need is Eno's Fruit Salt. Works like a charm.

ROBERTA: *(To JAMIE.)* You've been at them again.

JAMIE: I'm not allowed to read the news. What's left but advertisements?

LOGAN: Did I smell pie or was I dreaming?

ROBERTA: They're in the summer oven. They'll be a little late.

CLAIRE: Not too late, I hope. *(With a glance at BOHDAN.)* We have to leave at quarter past.

LOGAN: Where you off to tonight?

CLAIRE: There's a card party down at the school.

LOGAN: You like cards, do you, Bohdan?

BOHDAN: Not the kind they play down there. *(Glances at CLAIRE.)* I'll just sit and watch.

JAMIE: That will suit Claire to a tee. She loves an audience. *(Pointed.)* Must be a womanly thing.

CLAIRE: What do you know about women?

JAMIE: You'd be surprised.

ROBERTA: Aloysius, how are you doing? Can I pass you anything?

ALOYSIUS: (*Wipes his mouth.*) Not at the moment, thank you.

ROBERTA: It's nice to have a full table again. The food always seems to taste better.

> *This remark conjures up the missing. For a moment, silence falls.*

LOGAN: You look pale, Anna.

ANNA: Do I?

JAMIE: (*Quoting from an advertisement.*) You who are pale, haggard and irritable—get your blood examined for iron deficiency!

ROBERTA: Jamie.

JAMIE: I'm only pointing out: it's the *blood*. (*To ANNA.*) Understand?

ROBERTA: That will do.

JAMIE: (*To ROBERTA.*) There's more where that came from.

ROBERTA: Spare us.

LOGAN: (*To ROBERTA.*) Think it's Anna we've over-worked.

ANNA: Not at all.

ROBERTA: Maybe she's missing C.L. I'm sure he's missing her. It must be lonely for him—rattling around that empty house.

ANNA: He's hardly ever there.

ROBERTA: Not while you're away, I suppose.

ANNA: Even when I'm home. He's been run off his feet.

LOGAN: *Our* doctor says the same. His patients have been coming down, he says, with the darnedest things— since the start of prohibition. Especially things that can only be cured by a little prescription for brandy.

ROBERTA: Very funny, dear.

LOGAN: Thought I'd get a rise. Should have warned you, Bohdan. Mrs. Reid is a full-fledged member of the WCTU. Know what that— [stands for?]

CLAIRE: *(Overlapping.)* Father!

LOGAN: Women Constantly Torment Us. It's something to keep in mind.

> *Pause.*

BOHDAN: That was quite a trick they played on us, the WCTU. Shipped us off to France, then pushed through prohibition. Left us high and dry. That was a joke that went around. Nobody laughed then, either. In fact, it was a grim day—the day we got the news. We wanted to be dry, all right. God, did we want to be dry! Only what we wanted was—not that kind of dry.

> *Beat. Puzzled stares at BOHDAN.*

They're fighting in a swamp.

ANNA: Why?

BOHDAN: *(Without meeting her eyes.)* Why! That's the first question you learn not to ask. I'll have more spuds, if there's any left.

ROBERTA: Here. *(Passes him a bowl.)*

ANNA: *(Suddenly.) I write from a landscape more romantic and pathetic than words can describe. My candle is stuck on a bayonet. Drops of water fall down onto my nose. I* knew it rained. But it hadn't occurred to me they were fighting in a swamp.

ROBERTA: Rosa has mentioned it—in her letters. She can't knit to save her soul. Her hands are all thumbs. So she travels into London, every other week, to serve hot tea at the stations—to the troops coming back on leave.

ANNA: And?

LOGAN gives ROBERTA a warning look.

ROBERTA: They're sometimes muddy.

ANNA: *(Abruptly, to ROBERTA.)* May I read her letters?

ROBERTA: I'm afraid you'll find them dreary.

CLAIRE: That's not the word I'd use.

LOGAN: Full of piss and vinegar!

ROBERTA: Logan.

JAMIE: Germans are swine. Austrians snakes. What she calls the Turks I wouldn't repeat at the table. And Americans? Slackers and poltroons! Makes you wonder what she's hiding— *(Glances at ANNA.)* —that aunt of mine.

ROBERTA: Leave poor Rosa alone. It's almost on her doorstep, after all. She can even hear the guns at night.

ANNA: All that way?

ROBERTA: Everything's in short supply. Flour, sugar, eggs. She found a recipe—

ANNA: It must be overwhelming to be in the midst of them. *(To BOHDAN.)* Is it?

CLAIRE: *(A warning.)* Aunt Anna.

ANNA: It's such a simple question.

BOHDAN: *(Without meeting her eyes.)* Where I come from they
               say: give to a pig when it squeals and a woman
               when she asks, you'll end up with a fine pig and a
               bad woman.

               A brief silence.

ROBERTA: She found a recipe—

ANNA: *(To BOHDAN.)* I'm asking how loud it is.

               *BOHDAN shakes his head. He wipes his hand
               across his mouth.*

BOHDAN: The smell was worse.

ROBERTA: She found a recipe for making a pound of butter out
               of half a pound—with milk and a little salt. You'd
               think she'd found a recipe for making gold!

ANNA: *(To BOHDAN.)* The smell of what?

BOHDAN: Whatever. Mustard gas, chloride of lime. Smoke
               and creosote, sweat and excrement. Putrefaction.
               Mostly putrefaction. The bread we ate, the water
               we drank, the clothes we wore, everything we set
               a hand on—stank of that. The earth is stuffed with
               corpses and—between the shells and the rain—
               they keep turning up. Great for the rats, of course.
               Rats will eat anything, but what they really seem to
               prize—are the liver and the eyes.

               Shocked silence. ROBERTA stands.

ROBERTA: *(To BOHDAN.)* Was that strictly necessary?

LOGAN: Roberta—

ROBERTA: Please don't interrupt. *(To BOHDAN.)* You had to
               do that, didn't you? You couldn't resist. You sit at
               my table—court my daughter—why?! When you
               resent us so much.

CLAIRE: Mother!

BOHDAN: *(To ROBERTA.)* I'm sorry.

ROBERTA: I've had your number from the start, Bohdan Stefaniuk. I know exactly what you are. You're nothing but a slea—

LOGAN: *(Stands.)* Roberta! Check on the pies!

> *ROBERTA exits.*

CLAIRE: *(To ANNA.)* This is your fault.

LOGAN: That's enough out of you.

CLAIRE: I told you, but you wouldn't listen.

> *CLAIRE stands and moves away. LOGAN sits.*

BOHDAN: *(With a glance at ANNA.)* It can't be done, you see? It always ends in trouble.

ANNA: If you don't know when to speak and when to keep your peace.

BOHDAN: You pushed me.

ANNA: No.

BOHDAN: Tak! [Yes!]

ANNA: Why? What kind of man truly enjoys doing a thing like that?

> *BOHDAN stands abruptly. He can hardly contain himself. He turns to LOGAN.*

BOHDAN: Do you object to my seeing your daughter?

LOGAN: No.

BOHDAN: *(To CLAIRE.)* I'm going to harness up. *(To LOGAN.)* We're working tomorrow?

LOGAN: *(Shakes his head.)* Day of rest.

BOHDAN: Monday morning, then.

BOHDAN puts on his cap and exits.

ALOYSIUS: Fifty-three years! That's how long it's been since I rode away from it. I saddled my horse at Cold Harbor on a night in June. Climbed on and headed northwest. Rode until I couldn't bear to ride another mile. How many months had I wandered? I couldn't have said. I looked around and there was no one. Not that I could see. I got off, unwrapped my fiddle. Had a notion I'd stand there, under a bowl of stars. Play 'til my fingers bled. But I couldn't tune it. Couldn't see to—seem to— *(Breaks off; gets himself in hand.)* For years I was mostly alone. Then they started to come. *(To LOGAN.)* You were among the first. What if it had been someone else, someone I couldn't like? But it was you, and you asked for help, and I gave it, and I stayed. I forgot to be fearful, you see. And, sure enough, in the fullness of time, it caught up to me. *(Beat.)* Young Bohdan is now where I was then. Fifty-three years ago. He thinks he can leave it behind. *(Stands; turns to LOGAN.)* Thank Mrs. Reid for supper.

LOGAN: I will.

ALOYSIUS starts off. CLAIRE runs after him and hands him his cap. He exits.

JAMIE: *(To LOGAN.)* Did you know?

LOGAN: He told me.

JAMIE: When?

LOGAN: I don't know. Years ago.

JAMIE: And you kept it to yourself? Or you told Geordie and Will. You did, didn't you?

LOGAN: Not by a long shot on a rook's eye.

JAMIE: Cold Harbor! What a bloodbath.

CLAIRE: Stop it, Jamie.

JAMIE: Seven thousand men slain in less than twenty minutes. They said the battlefield—

CLAIRE: *(A warning.)* We don't need to hear this, Mutt.

            JAMIE glances at CLAIRE, then at LOGAN.

JAMIE: No. God forbid we should talk about anything that matters.

            JAMIE stands and exits.

LOGAN: Do me a favour, lass. Slip out there and see if you can hustle those pies along.

            CLAIRE throws a glance at ANNA and exits.

            What's going on here, Anna?

ANNA: *(Shrugs.)* Roberta's right. He's got a chip on his shoulder.

LOGAN: Annie.

ANNA: All I did was ask a question.

LOGAN: I think you were goading him.

ANNA: *(Stands.)* Well, maybe he deserved it. *(Begins piling dishes.)*

LOGAN: I don't know how you can say that after what he's done for us.

ANNA: Slaughter a pig, you mean?

LOGAN: He told the recruiters his name was Smith. They wouldn't have taken him otherwise. A man who wants to fight that much deserves a little respect. In my house—at my table—that's what he's going to get.

            ANNA stops piling dishes, but doesn't reply.

I'll be telling Roberta the same thing—if she ever comes back with my pie.

ANNA exits. LOGAN stares at his hands.

Scene Two

The verandah. Late that night. The screened door opens and ROBERTA, wearing a dressing gown and carrying a lantern, steps onto the verandah. She peers into the distance. ANNA enters suddenly from the yard.

ROBERTA: Good Lord, you scared me half to death! What are you doing out here?

ANNA: Prowling around.

ROBERTA: Whatever for?

ANNA: I couldn't sleep.

ROBERTA: Who can, after— *(Catches herself; breaks off.)*

ANNA: Yes. *(Sits on the steps.)* It's awfully still, isn't it?

ROBERTA: The barometer's falling.

ANNA: That isn't good.

ROBERTA: Let's hope it's only rain. And only a little of that.

In the distance, a coyote howls. ROBERTA shivers.

I'll never get used to that. *(Turns to go.)* Well—

ANNA: Roberta— *(Breaks off.)* Would you sit with me?

ROBERTA: Not if you're going to—

ANNA: Just 'til we hear the buggy.

ROBERTA sits reluctantly. She sets the lantern between them.

ROBERTA: She promised they'd take Sarah home. But it's three miles between there and here...

ANNA: It's a lovely night to be out. *(Stares off.)* You're lucky to live here.

ROBERTA: Am I?

ANNA: *(Surprised.)* Aren't you?

ROBERTA: I never stop thinking of home. Never stop missing it.

ANNA: You don't let it show.

ROBERTA: I have Kipling's antidote, tucked away upstairs: a handful of soil. *(Recites.)* Take of English earth as much/ As either hand may rightly clutch.../ Lay that earth upon thy heart,/ And thy sickness shall depart!

ANNA: And does it?

ROBERTA: *(Very dry.)* Not when it's thirty below. *(Stares off.)* Sometimes I think we're both half mad. He came because of a book. William Butler's *The Great Lone Land*. It set his brain on fire. Had he ever seen the back end of a cow? Was I any wiser? I made up my mind to like it. But it's too big for me, too—feral. The winters are savage, and the summers—

ANNA: I had to come back here. I had to. The house was so empty, you can't imagine. I thought I'd go out of my mind. *(Turns to her.)* I'm grateful to you for letting me come. I know I'm not easy to have around. I can be a loose cannon—

ROBERTA: Stop.

ANNA: I'm chock full of—chock full—I'm— *(Breaks off.)* What to do with it, where to put it: this I can't seem to work out. *(Several beats.)* I was afraid I'd never have a child. All those miscarriages. Then, at last,

Alexander. Such a difficult birth. For what? To lose him at seventeen? What kind of God turns his face away? Is He grieving, too—or ashamed?

ROBERTA: That's a terrible thing to say.

ANNA: Is it?

ROBERTA: Yes.

ANNA: You would never feel that way.

ROBERTA: I certainly hope not.

ANNA: You have three others, though.

> *ROBERTA stands abruptly and moves to the screened door. A dog barks, off. In the distance, a wagon is heard approaching.*

Roberta?

> *ROBERTA turns back. She is barely in control.*

ROBERTA: You can't undo what's done. Find the strength to accept that. If you don't have the strength within yourself, for God's sake pray for it! And pray for solace, while you're at it—like the rest of us. His mercy is infinite. I imagine it extends to you. *(Opens the screened door.)* You'd better not let her catch you here—if you know what's good for you.

> *ROBERTA exits through the screened door. The buggy draws closer, harness jingling, and comes to a stop, off. ANNA moves to the screened door and opens it.*

BOHDAN: *(Off.)* Won't you even say goodnight? Claire?

> *ANNA closes the door quietly and retreats into the shadows. CLAIRE comes striding on. BOHDAN follows her. He catches her hand and stops her.*

I said I was sorry. I'll say it again. I've forgotten

how to behave. I should have played a hand or two—

CLAIRE: It isn't that.

BOHDAN: What, then?

CLAIRE: You sat and brooded all evening. Almost as though you were sneering at us. Is that what you are, a cynic?

BOHDAN: I wasn't brooding, I was thinking.

CLAIRE: Yes, about her. Admit it!

BOHDAN: Claire—

CLAIRE: *(Pulls her hand away.)* Why? Why even talk to her?

BOHDAN: I don't have much choice.

CLAIRE: What an answer!

BOHDAN: I don't.

CLAIRE: Ignore her. Walk away from her. Pretend she doesn't exist. I don't know what hold she has over you, but the sooner you break it, the better.

BOHDAN: *(Sighs.)* All right.

CLAIRE: *(Surprised.)* Really?

BOHDAN: Really. Now what's wrong?

CLAIRE: I don't think you're serious.

BOHDAN: Don't do this, Claire. Don't stoop to this.

CLAIRE: What do you mean, don't stoop? I don't understand you at all! You spill out all that— ugliness, right at the supper table. Then when there's only the two of us, you haven't a word to say. All you do is look at me—

BOHDAN: I like to look at you. I'd forgotten there was anything—I'd almost begun to think— *(Breaks off.)* You're lovely to look at, that's all. Like sunlight through amber. My mother had a vase the colour of amber, that she—it was— *(Breaks off again.)* Beautiful, the shape. Delicate. When she held it up the window— *(Beat.)* —it glowed like a piece of the sun. I thought about that vase a lot, when things got bad over there. I'd have thought of you instead, if I'd known you then. Just as well I didn't. *(Two beats.)* I'm not sure this is a good idea.

CLAIRE: What do you mean?

BOHDAN: I'm almost afraid to touch you. I don't want you to shatter—

CLAIRE: I won't.

BOHDAN: I've turned a bit rough, you know, I'm—

> *She suddenly kisses him. Then she steps back. He stares at her, stunned. She runs up the verandah steps and disappears inside. He turns and sees ANNA. Their eyes meet. She slips through the screened door and disappears inside. After a moment, he exits. We hear him lead the horse and wagon away.*

Scene Three

> *The barn. The following morning: Sunday. A rooster crows. Sparrows make a racket in the loft above. LOGAN sits on a wooden stool, polishing his shoes. He is dressed for church. On a stool beside him lies a sweater.*

LOGAN: Browband, winkerbrace, blind. Nose strap, bit strap, bit. Bridle cheek, throat lace, crown.

> *ANNA enters unseen, with a camera.*

Breast strap, pole strap—? Hame! *(To the sweater.)* Well done! There's a rhythm to it, you see? You have to get into it. Breast strap, pole strap, hame. Collar strap, trace safe, belly band. Back band, back strap, collar. Come, lad, pay attention. You can't be saying *that piece there* when there are twenty-some. Rump safe, quarter strap, trace. Lazy strap, hip strap—

ANNA: Logan?

> *LOGAN leaps up in embarrassment. He tucks the sweater away.*

What are you doing?

LOGAN: Nothing.

ANNA: What were you saying?

LOGAN: Harness. Parts of a—parts of a harness.

ANNA: Whose sweater is that?

LOGAN: *(Beat.)* Geordie's. *(Sits.)*

ANNA: *(After a moment.)* Logan. *(With infinite pity.)* Oh, Logan—!

> *LOGAN can't meet her eyes. He busies himself with his shoes.*

It's hateful, isn't it? Hateful! What it's done to us.

> *LOGAN spits on a shoe. He takes his time.*

LOGAN: But it straightened William out. Which is more than I could do. He was all rough edges, was William. Hot-tempered, too. He whacked Jamie with a fork when we were haying one day. Whacked him solid across the head. Scared the hell out of us. Now he seems to have found his way. God knows, I'm glad of that. *(Beat.)* Geordie had a temper, too, but he was never mean. A bit of a hell-raiser. Don't know how I got such sons. They're none of them much like me.

ANNA: You mustn't let Jamie go.

LOGAN: He could walk down the line tomorrow and lie about his age. They'd hardly turn him away. I know it, and he knows it.

            ANNA begins to pace.

ANNA: We ship off what's most precious—and what do we get in return? A scrap of paper, just a—scrap of paper! A few cryptic words.

LOGAN: *(Overlapping.)* What brought you down here, Anna?

ANNA: His letters were cryptic, too. Full of contradictions. *I often pass close to bodies that are collapsing back into the clay. This is more comforting to me, this honest return to mother earth, than the poverty of a funeral, the coldness of a casket —*

LOGAN: Anna, for the love of Christ! Give it a rest, would you?

            Pause. They exchange a smile. ANNA glances around.

ANNA: Listen to those sparrows! I'd forgotten the racket they make. I thought I'd find Trooper here.

LOGAN: He's out in the pasture. *(Gives her a look.)* Hope you're not thinking what I think you're thinking.

            ANNA takes a pistol from a nail and examines it.

ANNA: I'm a good rider, Logan.

LOGAN: Not good enough.

ANNA: *(Shudders.)* Have you ever seen anything so

ugly? *(Puts the pistol back; resumes moving.)* It's hollow-sounding, isn't it? An empty barn. Like a mausoleum.

LOGAN: *(Shakes his head.)* Budge. Had a horse like you once. She never did what she was told to, either. She was half of my very first team. Fuss and Budge. What a pair they were. Fuss was worth his weight in gold. Could he lean into the collar!

ROBERTA enters unseen.

Budge wasn't worth what she dropped behind her. I don't mean that about you. But I never knew a horse so stubborn. She was born with her mind made up. Used to call her Won't Budge—and a few other names besides. Nearly wore my lungs out, swearing at her.

ROBERTA: I see you're at it again.

LOGAN chooses to misunderstand. He glances down at his shirt. There's a smudge of shoe polish on it.

LOGAN: Oh hell, Roberta. I'm sorry.

ROBERTA: Are you?

LOGAN: Well, maybe I'm not. Maybe by now you should know. I never think of my shoes of a Sunday until I'm nearly dressed. If I put them on first, I'd think of them first. That's not possible.

ROBERTA: That wasn't what I meant. I think you know it, too.

ANNA: It's my fault, Roberta. I love to get him talking.

ROBERTA: Talking is one thing, ruminating is another. There's no good comes of that. Why don't you come with us? It might help you.

ANNA: I want to take some more photographs.

ROBERTA: Of bones, I suppose. It's no wonder you're in the state you're in. Look where your mind is at!

ANNA: I find them intriguing.

ROBERTA: Intriguing! Well, I'm sorry, that's beyond me. *(To LOGAN.)* I'd like you to wake your daughter.

LOGAN: My daughter. Ah. Late again.

ROBERTA: There won't be a choir without her.

ANNA: I'll do it, Roberta. *(Starts off.)*

ROBERTA: If you dare. Give Jamie a shout while you're at it. He just went up to change.

ANNA exits. LOGAN sits to put on his shoes.

LOGAN: I've been thinking, Roberta. I've done quite a bit of thinking and I've made up my mind. If I want to talk to my sister about horse foibles or horse shit or any other goddamned thing, I'm going to do it. That's the way it is. So there's no use grumbling about it.

ROBERTA: I'm only thinking of you.

LOGAN: You don't need to think of me. I'm fine, Roberta, fine! I've never been so goddamned fine. Wish you'd stop worrying. I'm going to hitch the buggy.

ROBERTA suddenly sits in his lap and hugs him.

ROBERTA: Precious.

LOGAN: *(Holding her.)* What's this for?

ROBERTA: I'll think of something. *(Straightens his tie.)* If you and I start fighting with each other…

LOGAN: We won't, Pet. We won't.

They stand.

ROBERTA: I found a dress in the burning barrel. What was left of it. Anna's.

LOGAN: What's that supposed to mean?'

ROBERTA: I don't know.

> *He studies her face, then exits. ROBERTA exits.*

Scene Four

> *The coulee. Several hours later. Thunder rumbles in the distance. ANNA is digging bones from the bank. There is a basket beside her and, behind her, a camera with a shoulder strap. BOHDAN enters quietly. He picks up the camera.*

BOHDAN: Does this belong to you?

> *ANNA starts.*

ANNA: No, the fairies left it. Of course it belongs to me.

BOHDAN: I've always wanted one of these.

ANNA: That doesn't surprise me.

BOHDAN: Oh?

ANNA: They're very aggressive.

BOHDAN: Cameras?

ANNA: Predatory. You see people as they never see themselves. Sometimes it feels indecent.

BOHDAN: Indecent! You don't know what indecent is.

ANNA: Why don't you tell me, then?

BOHDAN: *(Avoiding her eyes.)* It sure isn't taking photographs.

ANNA: *(Resumes work.)* I did portraits of my son's friends, before they left. I couldn't resist.

He trains the camera on her.

Now I have all the negatives. You'd be surprised what you discover when you really study them.

He takes her photograph. She turns on him.

You shouldn't have done that.

BOHDAN: I had to test your theory.

ANNA: *(Faces him.)* Give me the camera, please.

BOHDAN: Why don't you come and get it?

ANNA: Bohdan.

BOHDAN: You said you weren't afraid of me.

ANNA: I'm not.

BOHDAN: Then come and get it.

She resumes her work. He shakes his head.

Stubborn. As usual. And still digging. I advised you to leave it alone. You're disturbing something that's been there maybe thousands of years. Doesn't that bother you?

ANNA: *(Stops work; faces him.)* What are you doing here?

BOHDAN: I saw you riding off. What a sight. Didn't anyone tell you you couldn't handle that horse? Though I have to admit, you tried. It's a wonder you stayed on him, the way you were bouncing around. What have you done with him?

ANNA: He's just down the coulee, helping himself to lunch.

BOHDAN: You hobbled him, I hope.

ANNA: Is that why you followed me? To see if I'd hobbled my horse?

BOHDAN: It's going to storm. He's very high-strung.

ANNA: Answer the question, Bohdan.

BOHDAN: *(Lightly.)* I came to apologize.

ANNA: For what?

BOHDAN: For what. For what I did at supper.

ANNA: Not for dousing me with blood and guts.

BOHDAN: *(Emphatically.)* That was between you and me. *(Turns away.)* But I shouldn't have opened my mouth last night. I don't know why I did.

ANNA: Oh, I think you do.

BOHDAN: *(Turns back.)* Look! When someone apologizes, you're supposed to be gracious about it.

ANNA: Thank you for the lesson in etiquette. *(Goes back to work.)* I'm not the one you should be speaking to.

BOHDAN: You mean Mrs. Reid. It wouldn't matter what I did, she'd soon find fault with it. *(Abruptly, watching her.)* Mrs. McGrath.

             ANNA looks up from her work.

             I could fall in love with you.

ANNA: *(Beat.)* No, you couldn't.

BOHDAN: Oh yes, I could.

ANNA: That would be a huge mistake. I have a husband—

BOHDAN: So you tell me.

ANNA: And there's Claire.

BOHDAN: Claire is a sweet girl—

ANNA: Very.

BOHDAN: I don't have to be seeing her. I could call a halt to that.

ANNA: *(Beat.)* I wish you hadn't said that.

BOHDAN: *(Moves closer.)* You smell of fear.

ANNA: No, I don't.

BOHDAN: All right. You smell of sage—and horse sweat.

ANNA: May I have the camera now?

BOHDAN: Sure you can. For a kiss.

                ANNA moves away.

             You won't loosen up, will you? I told you you should to learn to flirt. I meant it, too. You'd be surprised what you could accomplish if you played along a bit. *(Moves closer still.)* Or maybe you've changed your mind. You don't want to know any more. You caught a whiff of the battlefield and now you're on the run.

ANNA: That's not it at all.

BOHDAN: Then why don't you pelt me with questions? Beg, cry, plead? I was starting to enjoy that.

ANNA: *(Stops work.)* Listen, I made you an offer. I offered you—

BOHDAN: Pity.

ANNA: That's right.

BOHDAN: Offer me something I want. Maybe we'll get somewhere.

ANNA: Bohdan—

BOHDAN: *(Abruptly.)* How can there be beauty where a friend lies dead? I have an answer for you. He'd been trudging through mud and entrails. He'd shared his food with vermin. If he'd seen the sky at all that night, it was like something crazed. To come across a white body, splendid under the moon—that would be purity. So he lay beside it, as a kind of homage. Which is what it deserved.

> *He drapes the camera over her shoulder. His hands linger on her arm.*

I'd like to lie beside your body. Mrs. McGrath.

> *She takes a step back. Thunder rumbles, closer.*

And I'd like that photograph.

ANNA: I won't develop it.

BOHDAN: It might be a dandy.

ANNA: I'll destroy the negative.

BOHDAN: *(Shrugs.)* Suit yourself.

ANNA: I will.

BOHDAN: *(Smiles.)* Your husband is a lucky man. I don't suppose you have a sister? That's a joke. I'd like to see that smile again. I'd give quite a lot for that.

> *Thunder rumbles, even closer, followed by a crack of lightning. He glances up.*

It's getting close. We'd better go.

ANNA: I'm not finished yet.

BOHDAN: Well, I'm getting out of here. Would you like to kiss me goodbye?

ANNA: No.

BOHDAN: *(Laughs.)* I didn't say you could. I just thought you might have considered it. It looked as though you had.

He exits. She sets the camera down and resumes digging. More thunder, closer than before. She stops, looks at the sky, begins to lay bones in the basket. Thunder rumbles again, then suddenly isn't thunder anymore, but a herd of buffalo stampeding across the prairie. She is just setting a thigh bone into the basket when she hears the change. She drops to her knees. The air is filled with the sickening sounds of impact and bellows of pain as the buffalo tumble over the edge of the coulee and plunge downward to their deaths. She covers her ears and rocks. A hawk screeches: scree! scree! scree!

Scene Five

The verandah. That evening. Dusk. The chirping of crickets is the only sound to be heard. LOGAN is about to read a new letter from William to ROBERTA, CLAIRE, JAMIE and ALOYSIUS.

LOGAN: Is everyone ready? Here goes. *(Reads.)* July twenty-one. Dear Father. I'm writing because of Peg.

ROBERTA: Only Father?

ANNA appears like a shadow at the screened door.

LOGAN: *(Resumes reading.)* Remember the horse I told you about? I had to shoot her last night.

CLAIRE: Oh...

LOGAN: *(Reading.)* Worst thing I ever did. I feel like I took a knife to myself. Can't get it out of my head. I'd set off with her in a helluv— *(Catches himself.)* In a heavy rain. The roads were a mess. Halfway the Hun let loose.

ANNA opens the screened door and steps out.

Peg took a hit. Down she went. Tried to get up. Tried to get up again. I jumped off the limber and

slogged to her side. Both her forelegs were gone.
But ole Peg didn't know. She kept trying to stand.
Twisting and tossing her head. Making a sound I'll
never forget. I couldn't stand that sound. I grabbed
my rifle and shot her. She knew I was going to.

CLAIRE: Poor William!

ROBERTA: Better the horse than him.

ANNA: *(To herself.)* That sound!

LOGAN: *(Reading.)* Having to do that to Peg, it really sticks
in my craw. It's not the same with a man. Say he's
hung up on a wire in the middle of— *(Catches
himself.)* —middle of nowhere. Making a— *(Catches
himself again.)* —making a racket. A poor sod like
that who won't shut up, you can take your gun
and— *(Breaks off; clears his throat.)*

JAMIE: And what?

LOGAN: *(An obvious lie.)* He scratched something out there.

JAMIE: No, he didn't.

LOGAN: Don't contradict me, lad. *(Resumes reading.)* And
maybe you don't feel good or bad, it just had to be
done. Then there's a horse like—

> *JAMIE stands abruptly, grabs the letter and reads
> it.*

ROBERTA: Jamie!

> *JAMIE hands the letter back, turns and starts off.*

CLAIRE: Jamie?

ROBERTA: You can't miss the rest of it!

> *JAMIE wheels around. He's beside himself.*

JAMIE: I went to church this morning. Came home,
chased Trooper down. Filled the wood box, did

the milking. *Didn't* shoot my pistol. All I ask is the goddamned truth.

ROBERTA: James Meredith Reid!

JAMIE: I must be an idiot. Thinking I'll get it here!

> *JAMIE exits. Pause. LOGAN folds the letter.*

CLAIRE: *(To LOGAN.)* Isn't there any more?

LOGAN: I think the rest can wait.

ALOYSIUS: *(Stands.)* I'll say goodnight then.

> *ALOYSIUS puts on his hat and exits. It has grown quite dark. The sky has cleared. A harvest moon is rising.*

ANNA: I know that sound.

ROBERTA: What sound?

ANNA: The sound he said Peg was making—that he couldn't stand. I heard it—in the coulee this afternoon. It's awful; you want to—but you can't, too late, it's worked its way in. Throbs in your stomach, your chest. Like you're part of it, like it's—then you're—craziest thing!—it's almost as though—you realize— *(Breaks off.)*

ROBERTA: What are you on about?

ANNA: *(To herself.)* My God.

> *ANNA suddenly runs down the steps. She is limping a little.*

LOGAN: He did throw you. Thought as much. Are you all right?

ANNA: *(Turns back.)* Of course.

LOGAN: Where are you going?

ANNA: *(In confusion.)* I'm—

CLAIRE: Not to check on Trooper. What does she care about him?

LOGAN: Claire!

CLAIRE: It took all the men nearly an hour to catch him and calm him down. It could have ended badly.

LOGAN: She knows that. She's apologized.

CLAIRE: It's not as though she wasn't warned. She's utterly ruthless.

ANNA: Claire?

CLAIRE: I know who was with you in the coulee. And I know where you're going now. What a pair! I wonder who's more appalling.

> Beat. ANNA turns and exits.

LOGAN: Shame on you, Claire.

CLAIRE: *(Stands.)* You'd take her side in anything. *(Moves to the screened door.)*

LOGAN: Hang it all, somebody has to. She's nearly alone in the world!

> CLAIRE opens the screened door and disappears inside. The door slams shut behind her.

What's got into her?

> ROBERTA gives him a look.

LOGAN: Oh! *(Beat.)* But why is she blaming Anna?

ROBERTA: Logan, you can't be that blind.

LOGAN: *(Considers this.)* All I've seen between them is antagonism.

ROBERTA: *(Sighs.)* Something like that. *(Stands.)* Thank God
              Claire's out of it. *(Opens the screened door.)* I suppose
              you're going to tinker with the tractor.

LOGAN: No, I'm coming in.

ROBERTA: You are? It's licked you, has it?

LOGAN: Not on your life. I'll get the best of it yet.

              They exit through the screened door.

Scene Six

              *The barn. Moments later. BOHDAN, ALOYSIUS
              and JAMIE are sitting around a lantern, sharing
              a bottle of illicit liquor and going through the box
              of war souvenirs that Geordie sent to JAMIE.
              BOHDAN leans into the box and draws out a
              buckle.*

BOHDAN: Saw a lot of these buckles.

JAMIE: Did you?

BOHDAN: Standard issue, I think. *(Tosses it down; points.)*
              Collar hooks. Shoulder tabs. They come off neat.
              (Picks one up.) This was an officer.

JAMIE: How can you tell?

BOHDAN: Once you've seen them, you don't forget. *(Tosses it
              down; rifles through the box.)* Buttons. Buttons. *(Picks
              up a photograph; studies it.)* Why would he send you
              a photograph like this? *(Pockets it.)*

JAMIE: Hey!

BOHDAN: It's not for you. The dead deserve some dignity.

              *He picks up another buckle, examines it. ANNA
              enters unseen.*

This is a nice one. *(Reads.)* *Gott mit uns.* Not that day, He wasn't.

He tosses the buckle back in the box, looks up and sees ANNA just as the others do.

JAMIE: What!

ALOYSIUS: *(Stands.)* Mrs. McGrath?

ANNA: *(To BOHDAN.)* I need to talk to you.

BOHDAN: What about?

JAMIE: *(Stands.)* You shouldn't be here.

ANNA: Ribs, thighs, skulls. The bank is littered with them. Like a kind of—crazy collage. Who would have dreamed? It could be so beautiful. Carnage, that is. That's what he meant, isn't it? There's beauty at the heart of it. He saw that, didn't he?

ALOYSIUS: *(To ANNA.)* Let me walk you back.

ANNA: I suppose it's a matter of scale. The greater the slaughter, the more exquisite the beauty. One animal, a dozen: it wouldn't be the same. It's because there are thousands of them. The pounding of hooves, the chaos. All that force on the move! You hear them, feel the earth tremble. Smell the frenzy, the fear.

JAMIE glances uneasily at the men.

Something has been unleashed that can't—that has a mind of its own. Intoxicating in its power. You could get drunk on it, couldn't you? If you let yourself. Maybe you have to let yourself. As they tumble over the edge.

We hear a horse shuffling about in a stall. She turns to ALOYSIUS.

You must have seen it in the early days.

ALOYSIUS: It was mostly over by then.

ANNA: But—

ALOYSIUS: I'll tell you what I saw. A morning in early spring. I
              woke up and, much to my surprise, the prairie was
              white with snow. What I thought was snow. But
              when I looked closer I realized: it was bones. As far
              as the eye could see.

ANNA: My God. Where did they go?

ALOYSIUS: Shipped east. Fertilizer. Loaded plenty myself.

ANNA: Tell me about Cold Harbor.

BOHDAN: *(To ALOYSIUS, with his eyes on ANNA.)* Don't
              answer her.

ALOYSIUS: *(Beat.)* A couple of creeks. A crossroads.

ANNA: Please, Aloysius. I need to know.

BOHDAN: Trespassing. Trespassing!

ALOYSIUS: I was seventeen. I'd seen it all, I thought. Then came
              Cold Harbor.

ANNA: Go on.

ALOYSIUS: We dug in amongst the corpses. A battle, two
              years before. *(Not easily.)* We waited. Heard a great
              rumble. Wagons, horses, cannons.

BOHDAN: Easy, Aloysius.

ALOYSIUS: They came at us, wave after wave. Wave after
              wave, we laid them low. The sound gets inside
              you, the smell. We won, they said, but it sickened
              me.

ANNA: It sickened you. *(Stronger.)* It sickened you.

BOHDAN: *(To ALOYSIUS.)* Don't. She has no right—

ANNA: *(To ALOYSIUS.)* What are you saying? I'm wrong?

BOHDAN: *(Stands.)* Of course you're wrong. You know nothing! You don't even know yourself! You stand in a coulee and stare at the earth and think you've figured it out?

ANNA: Why can't I get through to you? I'm trying to understand—

BOHDAN: You can't!

ANNA: —why we keep doing this! How we can do it and walk away and do it all over again! There must be something I'm missing. Something that *you* know— *(To ALOYSIUS.)* —and *you* know—that nobody's telling me! *(Struggling.)* You—bring a child into the world. A son. You birth him and almost before you can breathe, he's off to the battlefield. Drawn like a moth to the— *(Breaks off.)* With a detour to the playing field. And no amount of love can—no— *(Still struggling.)* Why must it be this way?

ALOYSIUS: Let's go, Jamie-boy.

ALOYSIUS propels JAMIE forward. They exit.

ANNA: *(To BOHDAN.)* Tell me I'm right or tell me I'm wrong. But tell me, for the love of God! Something was there—in the midst of the horror—that lifted him out of it. Something! Why can't you help me with this? Why is it so much to ask? What is it that holds you back? Decency? Honour? Not likely. You can't be made to care. You're nothing but a brute. A savage. I won't ask you again.

She turns away. He grabs her roughly. He hits her.

BOHDAN: Don't ever call me that!

She is still reeling from the blow when he takes her face in his hands, kisses her provocatively, then

> *abruptly lets her go. She slaps him as hard as she can. He laughs.*

Is that the best you can do?

ANNA: You're a madman.

BOHDAN: Because of you.

ANNA: Insane! All you have to do is tell me!

> *He flings her to the ground. She gets up. She shoves him.*

Tell me! Tell me!

> *He shoves her back. She shoves him again. He shoves her up against a wall and moves in tight. He takes her throat in his hands. In his off-stage stall, Trooper begins to grow restive.*

BOHDAN: A twist of my hand!

ANNA: Do it, if that's what it takes.

BOHDAN: I think it's what you want.

ANNA: Do it! I dare you. But tell me.

> *His hands leave her throat to explore her face.*

BOHDAN: Say you want it. Say it.

> *His fingers wind through her hair. He pulls her toward him and kisses her passionately. She responds momentarily, then suddenly wrenches away.*

ANNA: Let go of me, you bohunk.

> *She pushes past him. He lunges at her. Both end up on the floor, rolling in straw and manure. What follows is an attempted rape/fight to the death. It should be unbridled, sustained, sexy and very physical. ANNA is fueled by her fear of/attraction*

to BOHDAN. He is much stronger, but his lungs are a mess. The more he exerts himself, the more difficult it is for him to breathe. Eventually, he's wheezing and gasping for air. ANNA finds herself, finally, against the wall where JAMIE's pistol hangs. She grabs it and fires at BOHDAN. The shot goes wild. He freezes, staring at her. From the stall come the sounds of a terrified horse. She fires again. The bullet tears past BOHDAN. He immediately reaches out to her. She drops the pistol.

ANNA: Oh my God—!

She sinks to her knees in shock. He leans against a wall and tries to calm his breathing. ALOYSIUS enters unseen.

BOHDAN: It's all right, Anna.

ANNA: No.

BOHDAN: It doesn't matter.

ANNA nods. ALOYSIUS slips out of sight.

We're hurt, we wail like dikooni. [wild men] We're scared, we shit our pants. When we have to defend ourselves—

ANNA shakes her head. We hear ALOYSIUS, off, trying to calm Trooper.

We're made that way.

ANNA: My God...

ALOYSIUS: *(Off.)* Steady, now. Steady.

BOHDAN: *(Not easily.)* What you don't want is to like it. Some of us do. More of us than you'd think. Put me in a room of men, I can pick them out. It leaves a mark on the iris. A permanent mark.

Pause.

The ones that snuff it are lucky. Alexander. You should be thankful he's gone. It's over for him forever. Then there's the ones like me. That aren't dead, but might as well be. Because once you get hooked on that kind of stuff, there isn't any escape. It comes and it puts its wild wild mouth— *(Struggles.)* —all over you. And everything that happens afterwards is just a gigantic yawn.

ALOYSIUS: *(Off.)* Hush. Hush, boy. Ssshh.

BOHDAN: Almost everything.

> *Pause.*

I guess you despise me now. Anna? Anna. Hanusia? [Dear Anna.] I've called you that in my mind.

> *ANNA has no response. A dog barks, off.*

Oh Christ. Leave me be.

> *She doesn't move. He turns on her.*

Leave me be!

> *ANNA pulls herself to her feet. Suddenly, LOGAN and JAMIE run on.*

LOGAN: What's going on here? Anna! Look at you!

ANNA: Logan, I— Logan, I—

LOGAN: Get Trooper out of here! Now!

> *JAMIE doesn't move.*

BOHDAN: It's my fault, Mr. Reid.

ANNA: No.

> *ALOYSIUS reappears. He moves next to BOHDAN.*

BOHDAN: She was just defending herself.

LOGAN: Against what?

BOHDAN: Against me.

LOGAN: Against—! *(Turns to ANNA.)* Is this true?

ANNA: Logan, I—wanted to kill him! And it felt—it felt—

BOHDAN: I'll pack my things and go.

LOGAN: You sure as hell will!

ANNA: No!

LOGAN: *(Beside himself.)* I can't have him around here now!

ANNA: I brought it on myself. I don't let up, you know that. I pushed him and pushed him and—then he pushed back. That's all there is to it.

LOGAN: Jesus Christ! What am I supposed to—

ANNA: Don't send him away, Logan, please. It was only ever between him and me.

LOGAN: Annie—

ANNA: Two adults, Logan. Two adults!

LOGAN: *(A desperate appeal.)* Aloysius?

BOHDAN: Fire me if you like, I don't give a—

ALOYSIUS: It's over now. It's done with.

LOGAN: You can't be sure of that.

ALOYSIUS: I'll vouch for him, Mr. Reid.

                Pause. LOGAN turns to ANNA.

LOGAN: Go up to the house. Tell Roberta what happened. Tell her everything. Did you hear me? Anna! Go.

> *ANNA exits. JAMIE picks up the pistol. LOGAN turns to BOHDAN.*

You stay away from her. Stay away from all of them. All of them, you hear?

> *LOGAN reaches for the pistol, but JAMIE exits with it. LOGAN follows him off. ALOYSIUS turns to BOHDAN.*

BOHDAN: Give me a minute. A minute.

> *ALOYSIUS exits.*

Scene Seven

> *The kitchen. The following day. Suppertime. ROBERTA and CLAIRE set food on the table. LOGAN, JAMIE, ALOYSIUS and BOHDAN enter and sit. The women sit. Heads are bowed. CLAIRE tries to sing grace, but can't. ALOYSIUS clears his throat.*

ALOYSIUS: If you'll permit me?

> *Heads are bowed a second time.*

For sun and rain, for fruit and grain / For friends we love so dearly / For gentle moments, kindly hearts / We thank thee, Lord, sincerely.

ROBERTA: Lovely. *(Passing ALOYSIUS a plate.)* For that, you deserve to start.

LOGAN: What is it tonight? Roast chicken? Well, better that than prairie chicken. *(To ALOYSIUS.)* Wouldn't you agree?

ALOYSIUS: *(Taking his cue.)* Unless it's cooked as it ought to be. Perhaps I've told you how. You put a prairie chicken in a pot of water. Salt it. Add a stone. Boil it for an hour and a half and then eat the stone.

ROBERTA: That might have been funny once, Logan—

> *ANNA enters and sits. No one looks at her but BOHDAN. She avoids his eyes. Pause. LOGAN clears his throat.*

LOGAN: Don't think you heard, Anna. The threshing crew comes tomorrow.

ANNA: That's good.

LOGAN: Now the real work begins.

ROBERTA: *(To ANNA.)* Pass me your plate. I'll fill it for you.

> *ANNA passes her plate. Another pause. LOGAN turns to CLAIRE.*

LOGAN: Saw a buggy come and go.

CLAIRE: Sarah. Art broke off their engagement.

LOGAN: Because of his legs.

CLAIRE: He won't say that. He claims he doesn't love her. She doesn't know what to believe. She says she can't seem to stop crying.

JAMIE: What she needs is nuxated iron.

CLAIRE: Jamie—

JAMIE: *(Quoting from a newspaper ad.)* Ladies, why not take nuxated iron and have nice rosy cheeks? The doctor gave some to Suzie Smith when she was sad and now she looks just fine.

ROBERTA: Jamie, you have a knack—

JAMIE: Don't I?

ROBERTA: For choosing the wrong moment.

JAMIE: *(Beat.)* Can't argue with that. *(Plays with his food.)* I'm fed up with them, anyway. I used to find them funny. Now I find them naive. They take us all for simpletons.

CLAIRE: Maybe that's what we are.

A silence.

LOGAN: You're not eating, Anna.

ROBERTA: She hasn't all day.

LOGAN: *(To ANNA.)* You'd better force yourself. As hard as you've worked since you got here, you'll be working much harder now. Roberta sometimes bakes all night. Don't you, Roberta?

ROBERTA: What choice do I have?

LOGAN: She has a reputation to uphold. Best food going, the threshers say. They're always happy to get here.

A dog barks, off. We hear a wagon approaching.

(To ANNA.) Come on now, eat up. We don't want C.L. complaining when he sees you that you're nothing but skin and bones.

ANNA: Oh, Logan, please!

ANNA shoves back from the table and stands so abruptly, a platter crashes to the floor.

ROBERTA: *(Stands.)* Oh, now look what you've done!

Louder barking, off. The wagon comes to a halt, off.

LOGAN: That'll be the foreman now. *(Stands.)*

JAMIE: Come with you?

LOGAN: No need.

LOGAN exits.

ROBERTA: *(To CLAIRE.)* Fetch the broom.

            CLAIRE stands and exits. ROBERTA kneels by the broken platter.

            My very best platter!

ANNA: I'm sorry.

ROBERTA: *(Begins to collect the pieces.)* Well, it's not the end of the world.

            CLAIRE returns with a broom and dustpan.

            Thank you, dear.

            ROBERTA begins to sweep up the pieces. LOGAN re-enters. He stands frozen in the doorway, a telegram in his hand. We hear the wagon move away. ROBERTA throws him a glance.

            Well? What did he have to say?

            LOGAN doesn't reply. ROBERTA turns to look at him.

            Logan?

LOGAN: *(Beat.)* William's been wounded, Roberta. Rather badly wounded, but he's going to live. He's been cited for bravery. He's coming home.

            Everyone falls still except ROBERTA, who continues to sweep. She sweeps and sweeps and sweeps. BOHDAN suddenly drops his head into his hands and begins to sob. ANNA turns to look at him. This is the moment when she should move to him. She doesn't. The others stare at him, astonished. CLAIRE turns away. ALOYSIUS moves next to BOHDAN and wraps his arms around him. Absolute silence, except for BOHDAN's sobbing.

Scene Eight

>*Exterior of the bunkhouse. A few weeks later.*
>*Overcast. From within the bunkhouse comes the*
>*sound of a fiddle. ANNA, dressed for travel, enters.*
>*Her camera hangs from her shoulder. She knocks on*
>*the door. The fiddle breaks off. ALOYSIUS opens the*
>*door and steps out.*

ANNA: I came to say goodbye.

>*ALOYSIUS takes her hand and bows.*

ALOYSIUS: You'll be taking with you the warmth of the sun.

ANNA: Always so gracious. Thank you. You'll look after
               them for me, won't you? They're going to have
               their hands full, once William gets home.

ALOYSIUS: They are.

ANNA: *(Releases his hand.)* Is Bohdan here, Aloysius?

ALOYSIUS: He's gone to see his father.

ANNA: Would you do me a favour, then? *(Takes the camera*
               from her shoulder.) Would you give him this? I want
               him to have it—and what's inside. It just needs
               developing.

>*ALOYSIUS accepts the camera.*

               And tell him when you see him— *(Breaks off.)* Tell
               him, please. I offered him something when I first
               met him—I found I couldn't give. Tell him I'm sorry
               for that. Tell him… the failure was mine. Tell him I
               think he was right: there are things you can't say in
               English. Or begin to explain. And tell him—I don't
               know, tell him—

ALOYSIUS: I'll tell him you're grateful to him.

ANNA: *(After a moment.)* I am.

ALOYSIUS: Who's taking you to Standfast?

ANNA: Mr. Reid. He's already hitched the horses.

ALOYSIUS: You'd better be going, then. I'll play you a song as you drive away.

ANNA: I'll listen for that, but I won't look back. You can't, can you?

> *ANNA exits. ALOYSIUS enters the bunkhouse and closes the door. A fiddle starts to play—a hauntingly beautiful tune. As we listen, the photograph BOHDAN took of ANNA appears in the distance. A hawk cries: scree! scree! scree!*

The End.

Relevant Dates

Anna, b. 1872, came to Canada 1895; m. C.L. McGrath 1896
Logan, b. 1857, came to Canada 1881; m. Roberta 1889
Roberta, b. 1862, came to Canada 1889
Claire, b. 1898
Jamie, b. 1902
Aloysius, b. 1847, came to Canada 1864
Bohdan, b. 1882, came to Canada 1891
William, b. 1890
Geordie, b. 1896, d. 1916
Alexander, b. 1900, d. 1917

American Civil War, 1861-65
1st Boer War, 1880-1881
World War I, 1914-18

Ukrainian Words and Expressions

Bohdan: pronounced with the emphasis on the last syllable. The "h" is pronounced like "h" in "horse."

To nicho: The "t" in "to" is pronounced like "to" in "torte." "Nicho" is pronounced "neecho" with the emphasis on the last syllable.

Nee: Pronounced like "knee."

Dumai: Pronounced like "Dubai" with the emphasis on the first syllable.

Durna: Pronounced "Doornah" (the -ah as in the word Ah!) with the emphasis on the last syllable.

Tak: pronounced""tack."

Yob tvoyou mat: The "t" is pronounced as the first "t" in "tuition.

Dikooni: The "i" is pronounced as in "hit" and the emphasis is on the last syllable.

Hanusia: Pronounced "Hanoosia" with emphasis on the second syllable.